CLINICAL SUPERVISION
OF PSYCHOANALYTIC
PSYCHOTHERAPY

CLINICAL SUPERVISION OF PSYCHOANALYTIC PSYCHOTHERAPY

Edited by
Jill Savege Scharff

KARNAC

First published in 2014 by
Karnac Books Ltd
118 Finchley Road
London NW3 5HT

British Library Cataloguing in Publication Data

A C.I.P. for this book is available from the British Library

ISBN-13: 978-1-78220-183-0

Typeset by V Publishing Solutions Pvt Ltd., Chennai, India

www.karnacbooks.com

CONTENTS

ACKNOWLEDGEMENTS

Introductory essay: We are grateful to Taylor and Francis for giving permission to modify Imre Szecsödy's article "Supervision should be a mutual learning experience." Reports and brief communications. *Scandinavian Psychoanalytic Review* 36(2) copyright © The Psychoanalytic Societies of Denmark, Finland, Norway and Sweden, reprinted by permission of Taylor & Francis Ltd, www.tandfonline.com on behalf of The Psychoanalytic Societies of Denmark, Finland, Norway and Sweden.

Chapter Five was derived, revised, and adapted from Govoni, R. M. & Pallaro, P. (2008). The supervision process in training. In H. Payne (Ed.). *Supervision of dance movement psychotherapy: A practitioner handbook* (pp. 33–48). London, UK: Routledge, with kind permission from Routledge. The authors wish to dedicate this chapter to the loving memory of Teresa Escobar whose contributions to the writing of this chapter they wish to recognize, along with those of Leonella Parteli and Marcia Plevin, faculty of Art Therapy Italiana (http://www.arttherapyit.org).

Elizabeth Rundquist dedicates Chapter Six in gratitude to her husband David Rogers.

In Chapter Nine, Christine Norman's use of an excerpt from the poem *Talk* by Kwame Dawes appears by permission of the author and courtesy of www.poet.org.

Chapter Ten appeared previously in *Refinding the Object and Reclaiming the Self* by David E. Scharff, (pp. 309–318) reproduced courtesy of Rowman and Littlefield.

Chapter Eleven appeared previously in *Tuning the Therapeutic Instrument* by Jill Savege Scharff and David E. Scharff (pp. 313–332) reproduced courtesy of Rowman and Littlefield.

ABOUT THE EDITOR AND CONTRIBUTORS

Carl Bagnini, LCSW, BCD, is a senior and founding faculty member at the International Psychotherapy Institute in Washington DC and in Long Island, NY, where his private practice is in Port Washington, NY. He is a clinical supervisor at the Ferkauf Graduate School of Psychology, faculty at The Derner Institute at Adelphi University and New York University Graduate Certificate Program in Child and Family Therapy. Mr Bagnini is a featured presenter at national and international conferences and videoconferences, and has written many papers and book chapters on object relations topics. His recent book is: *Keeping Couples in Treatment: Working from Surface to Depth* (Lanham, MD: Jason Aronson, 2012).

Joyce Y. Chen, PhD., is a clinical psychologist, China-licensed counselor, member of Shanghai International Mental Health Association (SIMHA), and member of Chinese Psychological Society for Professionals in Clinical and Counseling Psychology. She specializes in psychodynamic therapy for individuals and emotionally focused therapy for couples. Dr Chen received her doctorate in Clinical Psychology from East China Normal University in Shanghai, after studying in the Masters program of Marriage and Family Therapy at Bethel University in California, USA. She currently practices as a psychodynamic marriage and family therapist with private clinics and hospitals in Shanghai. Dr Chen holds certificates from the 3-year Sino-German Psychodynamic Psychotherapy training, the 2-year China American Psychoanalytic Alliance (CAPA) program, the 2-year Psychodynamic Couple Therapy training by David and Jill Scharff, the Satir Family Therapy Professional Training and the Emotionally Focused Therapy (EFT) training. She has published research in *Asia Pacific Journal of Counseling and Psychotherapy*, the *Chinese Mental Health Journal*, and the *Shanghai Archives of Psychiatry*, and currently writes a digital column for Chinese parents with young children.

Xiaoyan Katherine Chen, MA, has a Bachelors degree in Chinese Culture and Literature and a Masters degree in Psychology from East China Normal University (ECNU) in Shanghai. She is a licensed counselor in China. For the last eight years she has been a psychotherapist in the counseling center of ECNU and at the Linxi counseling center in Shanghai. She also has a private psychotherapy practice treating adults and adolescents. She is a graduate of the two-year China American Psychoanalytic Alliance (CAPA) training program and has been accepted into the two year advanced training program of CAPA. She is also a graduate of the three-year Chinese-Norwegian continual training project for senior psychodynamic psychotherapists. She has also trained as a Satir Model Family therapist. She supervises at ECNU and Linzi and also teaches at DRM Psychological Education for training counselors in Shanghai.

Rosa Maria Govoni is a psychologist, psychotherapist, and board certified dance/movement therapist. Dr Govoni works in different clinical settings, is faculty and supervisor in the Art and Dance/Movement Therapy training program at Art Therapy Italiana, as well as the Co-Director of the Expressive Psychotherapy Institute in Bologna, Italy.

Jaedene Levy, MSW, is a psychotherapist in Chevy Chase Maryland. In addition to her private practice with adults and couples, she is on the faculty of the Washington School of Psychiatry, guest faculty of the Washington Center of Psychoanalysis, and Fellow of the International Psychotherapy Institute. Mrs Levy is co-author of *Intimate Transformations* and *The Facelift Diaries*.

Christine C. Norman is a licensed clinical social worker who maintained a private psychotherapy practice in Salt Lake City, Utah for 18 years, treating adults, children and couples. Having taught oral English for the University of Nankai, in Tianjin, China from 2009–2011, she moved to Cochabamba, Bolivia (2011–2013) and currently lives in Oaxaca, Mexico. She is a Fellow of the International Psychotherapy Institute and was a founding faculty member of IPI-Salt Lake City and currently serves on the advisory board. She has been adjunct faculty for Brigham Young University in the Masters of Social Work program. She teaches and supervises for the China America Psychoanalytic Alliance (CAPA). She is co-author of *Intimate Transformations: Babies and Their Families* (2005; Italian, French, Spanish and Kindle editions).

Patrizia Pallaro, LCMFT, BC-DMT, is a bilingual licensed psychotherapist, board certified dance/movement therapist, writer and editor. She is a faculty member of Art Therapy Italiana, clinical supervisor and lecturer in the Dance/Movement Therapy Department of the Institute of Applied Psychology and Psychoanalysis in Moscow (Russia), and Fellow of the International Psychotherapy Institute. Mrs Pallaro maintains a private practice in Bowie, Maryland, where she offers individual, couple, family and group therapy.

Mary Jo Pisano, PhD, is a licensed clinical psychologist who practices psychoanalytic psychotherapy and provides clinical supervision for therapists. Her early years were devoted to family therapy treatment with drug and alcohol patients, and she now treats patients with a variety of complaints. Dr Pisano is on the faculty of the International Psychotherapy Institute in Chevy Chase, Maryland, and offers individual and couple therapy in the Pittsburgh area, where her private practice is now in its 30th year.

Elizabeth A. Rundquist, MA, ATR-BC, ATCS, is an art therapist trained at New York University and Fellow of the International Psychotherapy Institute. She worked for 17 years in the public mental health sector, taught at various colleges, and remains curious and continues to learn in seminars and study groups. Ms Rundquist has a small private practice where she works with cultural difference, the changing role of women, and the wish to live in harmony across generations.

Colleen Sandor, PhD, is a licensed psychologist in private practice of psychotherapy in Salt Lake City, Utah, where she works with adults and couples. She is Assistant Professor of Psychology at Westminster College where she teaches Master's in Counseling students. She is a faculty member of the International Psychotherapy Institute (IPI) and co-director of the Salt Lake chapter of IPI where she teaches and supervises clinicians.

David E. Scharff, MD, is co-founder and past director of the International Psychotherapy Institute (IPI); supervising analyst, International Institute for Psychoanalytic Training at IPI; Clinical Professor of Psychiatry, Georgetown University and at the Uniformed Services University of the Health Sciences; Teaching Analyst, Washington Psychoanalytic Institute; and psychoanalyst, couple and family therapist in Chevy Chase, Maryland. Dr David Scharff is the author of *The Sexual Relationship* and *Refinding the Object and Reclaiming the Self*; co-author of *Object Relations Family Therapy, Object Relations Couple Therapy, Tuning the Therapeutic Instrument* and *The Interpersonal Unconscious*; editor of *Object Relations Theory and Practice*; and co-editor of *Psychoanalytic Couple Therapy*. He is co-editor with Sverre Varvin of *Psychoanalysis in China*, and editor of the new journal *Psychotherapy and Psychoanalysis in China*.

Jill Savege Scharff, MD, is co-founder, International Psychotherapy Institute (IPI); founding chair and supervising analyst, International Institute for Psychoanalytic Training at IPI; Clinical Professor of Psychiatry, Georgetown University; Teaching Analyst, Washington Psychoanalytic Institute; and psychoanalyst, couple and family therapist in Chevy Chase, Maryland. Dr Jill Scharff is the author of *Projective and Introjective Identification and the Use of the Therapist's Self*; co-author with David Scharff of *The Primer of Object Relations (2nd edition), Object Relations Therapy of Physical and Sexual Trauma*, and *Object Relations Individual Therapy*; editor of *The Autonomous Self: The Work of John D. Sutherland* and *The Psychodynamic Image: The Work of John D. Sutherland on Self and Society*; and co-editor of *The Legacy of Fairbairn and*

Sutherland. Her most recent edited books are *Psychoanalysis Online* and *Psychoanalytic Couple Therapy*.

Imre Szecsödy, MD, PhD, is a training analyst and supervisor at the Swedish Psychoanalytic Society of which he was formerly Director (1989–1993) and President of the Swedish Psychoanalytic Society (1993–1997). He was vice president of the European Psychoanalytic Federation (EPF) (1997–2001) and member of COMPSED (committee of psychoanalytic education) of the IPA (2000–2004). He is an adjunct faculty member of the International Institute for Psychoanalytic Training at the International Psychotherapy Institute in Chevy Chase MD, USA. Dr Szecsödy has conducted extensive research into supervision and the learning process and has long experience of conducting formal training of supervisors. His doctoral thesis from the department of psychiatry at the Karolinska Institutet, St. Gøran's Hospital, Stockholm was published as *The Learning Process in Psychotherapy Supervision* (Private Press, 1990) and he co-authored with Irene Matthis *On Freud's Couch: Seven new interpretations of Freud's Case Histories* (Jason Aronson, 1998). Dr Szecsödy has published and presented extensively on supervision, most recently compiling the best of his papers in his e-book, *Supervision and the Making of the Psychoanalyst* (2013b).

Elizabeth H. Thomas, MSW, PhD, is a clinical social worker on the faculty of the New Directions Program of the Washington Center for Psychoanalysis. Dr Thomas maintains a psychotherapy practice for individuals and couples in Chevy Chase, MD and at her home in Bluemont, VA.

Chunyan Wu, MD, received her medical degree from Shanxi Medical University, Taiyuan, China. She is a registered and certificated clinical psychologist of Clinical Psychology and Counseling with the Chinese Psychological Society. She is currently an attending psychiatrist at Shanghai Mental Health Center. A member of the China American Psychoanalytic Alliance (CAPA) since 2007, she has graduated from the two-year certificate program. Since 2005, she has also studied with the Sino-German Psychodynamic Psychotherapy training in individual and group therapy.

INTRODUCTION

Jill Savege Scharff

The theory and practice of psychoanalytic psychotherapy supervision rests on concepts drawn from the analytic literature, research, and sound educational philosophy informed by analytic sensibility. The book begins with an introductory essay by Imre Szecsödy, drawn from his years of experience in preparing analysts to be supervisors and his commitment to research into that process. In Chapter One, Jill Scharff introduces the concepts of frame and focus, boundary and task that are essential in dealing with the ambiguity of the supervisory role. Appreciating the complexity of that role, the clinician who would like to become a supervisor prepares by attending reading seminars. Beginning the first supervision, the new supervisor attends individual and group supervision of supervision in which a secure, ethical setting allows for open, respectful communication. This offers a good holding environment that supports the supervisor and supervisee to develop a trusting relationship, a shared language, and a commitment to examining unconscious conflict in the supervisory encounter as well as the patient–therapist dynamics. Jaedene Levy follows with two case examples of work with supervisees who challenged the boundaries of the supervision frame and focus. One of them blurred the boundary and tried to reduce the authority of the supervisor by appealing to her to be a friend instead, and the other resonated with her patient's pain rather than confronting its underlying dynamics. Levy found detailed process notes useful in establishing frame and focus.

When a supervisee is treating a patient whose mind is in bits, the supervisor must contain a highly anxious supervisee in a turbulent system. Reflecting as a supervisor in the present on her experience as a supervisee with such a case in the past, Mary Jo Pisano describes how the supervisor successfully makes room for the therapist to express her anxieties, and thereby provides a model for containment that she can apply in her clinical work with patients. Many supervisees come to supervision looking for more than the supervisor expects to offer. Carl Bagnini shows how the tactful, responsible supervisor deals with unconscious motives yet avoids the trap of behaving like a therapist in response to a regressive pull. He describes his supervision with a woman who idealized him and preferred to engage him in discussion about various ways in which she could emulate his success as a clinician and teacher, rather than deal with the clinical work she was actually doing with her patient. He found that a self-imposed silence helped him to re-establish frame and focus.

Verbal and non-verbal communication is important in supervision as they are in psychotherapy. The next two chapters focus on bodily and artistic aspects of non-verbal communication. Rosa Maria Govoni and Patrizia Pallaro apply the concepts of psychoanalytic psychotherapy supervision based on object relations theory to supervision in Dance Movement Therapy, a treatment method in which movement, gesture, and dance inform understanding and intervention in individual and group settings. Elizabeth Rundquist does the same for art therapy, in which art is a creative, esthetic expression of unconscious thoughts, feelings, and internal object structures, and is a reflection of transference and countertransference in the intersubjective space.

Drawing on her extensive thesis on psychotherapy supervision, Elizabeth Thomas highlights and illustrates aspects of her qualitative, phenomenological research into social workers' experience of conflict in supervision. She describes the implications of her study for best practice of clinical supervision, not confined to supervisees from a social work background. A clear picture emerges of the qualities that characterize the good supervisor for any psychotherapist.

Two chapters address issues arising in group supervision. After reviewing trauma theory, Colleen Sandor describes a patient with a trauma history whose treatment the author discussed when she was a participant in a supervision group led by David Scharff. Sandor found that the group offered a broader context and stronger frame for coping with the terror of trauma than she might have found in individual supervision. Christine Norman and her three Chinese supervisees Joyce Y. Chen, Xiaoyan (Katherine) Chen, Chunyan Wu come together in a dialogue to address the impact of technology and the cross-cultural issues they faced teaching and learning psychotherapy via Skype in English.

One task of supervision is to work with what is often referred to as parallel process in the system consisting of patient, therapist, supervisor, and institution: The therapist's issues reflect or are triggered by those of the patient, are further reflected in the dynamics of the supervisory pair, and in the institution where supervisee and supervisor work. In his chapter on this topic, David Scharff addresses the therapist's resonance with the patient, and illustrates it in his work with a supervisee whose family therapy with a suicidal adolescent had triggered her own death constellation. He discusses the responsibility of supervisors to encourage supervisees to confront their own internal areas of loss, grief and fear in order to help their patients. The text concludes with Jill Scharff's description of her work with a supervisee in an institution where individual supervision is embedded in a learning matrix designed to support, and be supported by, the supervisee's growth and development. This supervisee was a pleasant person who was unable to resonate with the negative transference. In supervision, it emerged that this was because she could not believe that she mattered enough to have an impact on her patients. Once she was helped to accept that her way of being, and her ordinary comings and goings, affected them, evoked longing, and created distress and anger at times, she became able to recognize, gather, and interpret the transference–countertransference, as the centerpiece of therapeutic action.

The contributors approach task, boundary, focus, and interaction in supervision from multiple vertices—research, analytic sensibility, group process, bodily and artistic expression, and individual teaching and learning in clinical supervision.

Supervision as a mutual learning experience

Imre Szecsödy

The need for training to increase the competence of supervisors for psychotherapists and psychoanalysts has been recognized more and more. Yet only a few institutes around the world have organized such a training course. To encourage more psychoanalytic institutes and psychotherapy organizations to commence training of supervisors, Jill Savege Scharff and her colleagues at the International Psychotherapy Institute have written *Clinical Supervision of Psychoanalytic Psychotherapy*, a collection of chapters on theory and practice of supervision. As Jill Scharff writes in her introduction: "The contributors approach task, boundary, focus, and interaction in supervision from multiple vertices— research, analytic sensibility, group process, bodily and artistic expression, and individual teaching and learning in clinical supervision." The topic of supervision, including the question of how to ensure high quality supervision for psychoanalytic psychotherapist and psychoanalysts, is dear to my heart. I have been doing and studying clinical supervision, and promoting research and training for supervision, over many years in Europe. Jill Savege Scharff edited a collection of my essays in an e-book called *Supervision and the Making of the Psychoanalyst* (2013b), and now it is my honour to contribute the introductory essay for her edited book *Clinical Supervision of Psychoanalytic Psychotherapy*.

I hold that the primary task for supervision is to help trainees in psychotherapy and psychoanalysis comprehend the "system of inter-action" between therapist and patient. This also means that students in psychotherapy (or candidates in psychoanalytic training) have to be able to "step out" of the system of interaction they have with each patient, to be able to observe and understand it. This can be facilitated by the creation of a "formal system for supervision" (Szecsödy, 2013a). This means that trainee or candidate and supervisor agree not only on theories about development, psychopathology and psychotherapeutic technique, but also on the rules of their interaction, thus constituting the frame for their work. To establish the frame, the supervisor has to maintain the boundaries around the primary and specific task of supervision, by separating it from the trainee's task of conducting psychotherapy or psychoanalysis. Rather than giving support, advice and suggestions, the supervisor should encourage the supervisee to organize information actively. By consistently focusing on and helping the therapist to reflect on the combined interaction of patient (patient–therapist) therapist, the supervisor maintains the formal system and can enable the trainee to step out of and observe his or her own system of interacting with the patient. Doing so, the supervisor has also the opportunity to learn more about what is happening during supervision and how to encourage mutual learning. It is also most important to train supervisors and to continuously carry out research on it.

According to the Webster Dictionary, supervision is: "An oversee-ing, surveillance, to inspect, scrutinize, examine, to have control over, to manage, to direct, to conduct". It refers to a situation, where psychotherapeutic or psychoanalytic work, carried through by an inexperienced trainee, is done under the control, the surveillance of a senior ("controlling, directing, managing, and conducting") supervisor. The supervisor, as a member of a training institute, has not only a status, but also the power and responsibility to judge, evaluate and influence the status of the trainee. The Oxford Dictionary defines a student "as a person who is engaged or addicted to study", and a candidate: "as one who offers himself or is put forward by others as aspiring to be elected to an office, privilege, or position of honour"—as candidate means being clothed in a white toga (*Candida*), the attire of one who is aspiring for an office in the Forum Romanum (Ekstein-Wallerstein, 1958).

Nonetheless, the primary task for supervision is and should be, to provide optimal conditions for the supervisee to integrate her/

his experiences, theoretical knowledge and her/his personality for a competent participation in and handling of the psychotherapeutic or psychoanalytic situation and process. The aim is for the supervisee to acquire core competences enabling her/him to conduct psychotherapy or psychoanalysis independently.

There are some stable differences in the way supervisees and supervisors work together. These differences can be placed under the headings *cognitive, working or defensive styles* (Jacob, 1981). The *cognitive style* is an ever-present general influence in the screening and organizing process. The personality embodies stabilized dispositions of perception and cognition which define the cognitive style. Close to this, but not synonymous, is the *working style*. It differs according to how and what basic concepts are characteristically used and how they are integrated into the actual work situation. The so-called *defensive style* is the third way of supervising, which is related to the ways control is used (Jacob, 1981).

To provide conditions in which learning can develop is not easy and can be complicated by the supervisee as well as by the supervisor. Parallel to the wish to learn and change, there is the fear of the unknown and a tendency to stay with the accustomed and to remain untouched by change. The supervisor has to be prepared for and aware of all the ambiguities that are inherent in the supervisory situation. There is "a crowd present" in the supervisory room: a mentor, teacher, evaluator, judge, supervisor, future colleague, a staff member who is dependent on the supervisor's acknowledgement and successful development, as well as the supervisee who has to accept and carry a number of different roles. Thus, it is important to differentiate between the supervisee's interest in increasing knowledge and skill, on the one hand, and acquiring a profession, on the other. As a result of these two motivations, the supervisor can expect to be experienced as a teacher, tutor, mentor, someone to relate to, rely upon and identify with or as a judge; controlling in the interest of the body of professionals and as a delegate of the "institution". In this sense, the supervisor can be a rival to fight with, or submit to. These are more-or-less realistic expectations and experiences connected with the culturally defined roles and status of the participants. These roles obviously have great potential for satisfying unconscious fantasies and transferential scripts. The intriguing question is: is learning possible under such complex and conflicting conditions?

In 1980, I commenced a study at the Stockholm Psychotherapy Institute. The aim of this project was to gain a better understanding of the supervisory process and about learning connected with it. This search for a better understanding made use of direct observations of the interactions between trainee and supervisor during the supervisory process. This approach was closely related to the increasing ambition amongst researchers of psychotherapy, to use more directly observable data and to analyze recorded sessions and/or transcripts of these. The training is a postgraduate one: trainees have a degree in medicine, psychology, social work or nursing. Supervisors are senior staff members at the Institute. All trainees have undergone a therapeutic experience themselves, in the form of a training-analysis or psychotherapy. The psychoanalytically oriented psychotherapies conducted by the trainees had a once-a-week frequency. Trainees met their supervisors individually once a week. Every 5th supervisory session was audiotaped. Transcripts were made of the tapes for systematic study. The first recorded session was the 4th or 5th supervisory session between trainee and supervisor, leaving space to record 5 additional supervisory sessions before the summer break and a further 8 sessions from the 2nd year of training until termination. In the course of the 4 supervisions that were followed, trainees had an average of 56 sessions with their supervisors. 14 of these were recorded, resulting in 56 transcripts of recorded sessions for the study. At the end, all supervisors and trainees were interviewed about their experience of the study.

Summary of the research

Work between trainees and supervisors was often influenced by conflicts, presumably related to the ambiguity and complexity of the supervisory task. Defensive warding off of information was observable more-or-less continuously in the work of the trainees. Supervisors less often followed an explicit, consistent and consequent focus than was expected. Supervisors showed a predilection to deal with all learning problems by giving information and suggesting strategies to the trainee. It was possible to find observable and recurrent instances in the supervisory interaction that can be judged as optimal for learning. It was also possible to connect these instances with repetitive patterns in the supervisory interaction. Helping the trainees to review the context and reflect on the meaning of the therapeutic interaction, connecting their own reactions with their patients' activity and communication, could be considered as the main task of supervision. The continuous maintenance of boundaries around this task, keeping an equidistant position, encouraging the trainees to organize the information and focusing on the patient (patient–therapist) therapist *gestalt* constituting a mutative learning situation, often coincided with conditions that seemed to facilitate learning, irrespective of the type of learning problems.

But this is not the whole task. It is also essential to establish a clear frame in supervision. This frame has a stationary aspect (agreement on goals, payment, methods, general rules for supervision as well as for the supervised therapy) and a mobile aspect (the continuous, reflective review of the working together). It is suggested that a 3rd aspect be called the supervisory position, referring to the supervisor's continuous focus, from a "non-judgmental, neutral, equidistant position", on the trainee's interaction with the patient. To keep a continuous focus from this equidistant position constitutes the maintenance of boundaries around the primary task for supervision. By clearly keeping these 3 aspects of the frame, the supervisor can increase the occurrence of conditions that have been found optimal for learning.

Training of supervisors

The need to increase the competence of supervisors via training has become increasingly acknowledged; however, there are few organized training courses for supervisors. To encourage more institutes and organizations to commence training of supervisors, I shall give a detailed description of the goals and structure of training for supervisors. I will provide a model for how to evaluate the competence of supervisors, the learning difficulties of supervisees, and how to study the work of supervision, based on research.

Training of psychotherapy supervisors was established in Sweden 1984 and training of supervisors of psychoanalysis in 1989. During the 3 terms of the training, psychotherapy trainee and supervisor met every week. Supervisor and super-supervisor met every 2nd week. Seminars were conducted once a month.

The goals for training of supervisors were formulated based on the supervisor's ability to enhance the trainee's ability to:

- reflect on and understand her/his own motives for undertaking supervision: differentiate different motives such as to be trained, learn about learning, or gain status, compete, and fulfill illusions;
- form a learning alliance with the supervisee and establish a working platform for her/himself as supervisor;
- hold anxiety, establishing phase-specific security in the supervisory situation;
- encourage continuous reflectiveness about the ongoing therapeutic/ analytic process as well as of the formulation of educational diagnoses;
- focus on the mutuality of interaction between patient and therapist/ psychoanalyst, as well as trainee and supervisor, and learn how to focus on the patient/analysand—therapist/analyst interaction, trying to connect how this patient-analysand's personality, past experiences, conflicts, and transferential enactments are expressed in the interaction with this particular therapist-analyst and how she/he experiences this, reacts to it and interacts with the patient;
- deal with lack of experience, skill and knowledge, and/or defensive avoidance of information (creating dumb or blind spots) due to conflicts relative to the patient (*learning problems*) and those relative to the supervisor (*problems about learning*) described by Ekstein & Wallerstein (1958);
- deal with transference–countertransference issues in the therapeutic/psycho-analytic relationship as well as in the supervisory relationship;
- recognize the presence and effect of parallel processes;
- increase the dexterous use of theory and the capacity for self-reflection and evaluation and at the same time tolerate uncertainties and not knowing, without forcing the experience to fit within preconceived ideas and theories;
- understand and deal with the ever-present ambiguities in the supervisory situation, such as in the case of the supervisee, wishing to be a good enough therapist/analyst despite being an unskilled trainee; being related to as a real person as well as a person in different transference roles; exploring difficulties openly, while at the same time exposing frailties for evaluation; and in the case of the supervisor,

providing optimal conditions for training and at the same time safeguarding the patient´s need to receive optimal conditions for the ongoing therapeutic/analytic process (Szecsödy, 1990, 1994, 1997, 2003, 2008).

Evaluation of supervisors

Having organized more and more training courses to become supervisors, I identify 12 criteria on which to evaluate the supervisors. I carried out evaluations along these lines in the middle and at the end of training. We looked for a supervisor's ability to:

1. establish a platform for a very serious play that at the same time is a working relationship;
2. establish a working platform for her/himself;
3. use the platform that the super-supervisor was able to establish;
4. reflect on and recognize the different roles she/he is working in, in the organization of the supervisee, where the supervision is conducted as well as in the training organization;
5. reflect on and understand her/his own motives for undertaking supervision, to differentiate between different motives and goals of being trained, learning to gain status, to compete, to fulfill illusions;
6. make a pedagogic diagnosis and differentiate between problems due to lack versus due to conflict (dumbness and blindness);
7. follow and identify the process developing between patient therapist/analyst as well as trainee-supervisor;
8. contain and deal with the built-in ambiguities in the supervisory situation, without using primitive defenses;
9. hold anxiety, establishing phase-specific security in the supervisory situation;
10. give space for the supervisee to bring in her/his emotionally cathected experiences of the interaction with the patient;
11. tolerate uncertainties and not knowing, not forcing the experience to fit within preconceived ideas and theories;
12. explore and enjoy the very serious play of supervision.

The criteria which supervisors could apply for the evaluation of trainees might also be grouped into 12 categories, each indicating slightly different dimensions of judgement supervisors can use to reflect on their supervisees' competence, by asking themselves: Does this supervisee:

- wait in a receptive state, recognising that there is an unconscious level to the patient's associations (whether able to make sense of them and interpret them or not);
- accept a (negative) transference position assigned by the patient (or can recognise counter-action as such);
- interpret—whether interpreting transference links between past and present, or otherwise and dynamically transforming them, rather than behaving in explanatory, seductive or intrusive ways, and instead operating from within a context of being able to bear, sense and conceptualise unconscious links;
- convey a sense of unconscious sensitivity so that the supervisor can sense a subjective feeling of space, receptivity and creativity during the supervision;
- use psychodynamic/analytic theory to discuss or consider the work but in a way driven by experience at the session;
- think independently of the supervisor being neither slavish to the supervisor's ideas, nor oversensitive to critical comment;
- show self-analytic capacity, particularly if it is reflected in psychic movement with the patient;
- choose appropriate language for interpretations;
- show development and movement in key capacities;
- show actual improvement in the patient, reflecting the supervisee's clinical work;
- show potential for development;
- show talent?

To be able to study how supervisors worked (and inspired by the frame of psychoanalytic work described by David Tuckett in 2005), I formulated a *Frame for the study of supervisory interaction on psychoanalysis*, which can also be used for psychotherapeutic supervision.

Frame for the study of supervisory interaction

I suggest assessing the quality of the supervisory interaction along 4 dimensions.

a. *Participant-observational frame*. We observe:

- How the supervisor provides frame and interactional space for the supervisee and how the supervisee approaches it, and uses it.
- How the material is presented: notes, free narration, transcripts/tapes.
- What the main or recurring focus is during the session: describing and reflecting about the analysand; the interaction between analysand and candidate, the candidate's own experiences and reflections; the interaction between candidate-supervisor.
- How the supervisor and/or supervisee deal with the "material" (the narrative of the analytic sessions)—as if the narrative is still going on, is present and open, or as something in the past, distant, closed, finished.
- How the supervisor and/or supervisee approach the narrative: reflecting about it, raising questions, giving/finding answers, using examples, advice, and theory.
- How the supervisor–supervisee approach learning problems, resisting, clarifying, confronting, interpreting, supporting, criticising.
- How the supervisee uses supervision: submissively, defensively, support-seeking, curiously questioning, reflectively, receptively, giving feedback.

b. *The supervisory conceptual frame*. We observe:

- How the supervisor seems to conceptualise the learning and teaching process.
- How the supervisor meets the ideas of the supervisees, conveys how psychoanalysis and psychoanalytic psychotherapy work, and how the supervisor relates this with his/her own transformational theory.
- How the supervisor meets the candidate's ideas about how supervision works and reflects on his/her ideas about how supervision works.

c. *The supervisory interventional frame*. We observe:

- How the learning alliance is handled.
- How the supervisor works with the candidate's countertransference towards the analysand.

- How the supervisor works with the candidate's transference towards the supervisor.
- How the supervisor works with his/her own countertransference reactions.

d. *The evaluation frame.* We observe:

- How evaluation of the supervisor/supervisee situation is conducted: spontaneously, structured, one-sided, mutual.

Conclusion

The continuous maintenance of boundaries around the task of supervision, keeping an equidistant position, encouraging the trainees to organize the information, and focusing on the patient–therapist/supervisee–supervisor relationship constitutes a mutative learning situation that facilitates learning, irrespective of the type of learning problems. I have always emphasized the importance of training supervisors as well as the necessity for research on the supervisory process and for gathering more information on how to reach and maintain competence as a supervisor. That is why I am so pleased to write the introductory essay for this interesting book, focusing on different and important aspects of supervision. Taken together the various chapters exemplify the basic idea that the most creative way to supervise is to have very clear frames, a clear agreement between supervisee and supervisor how they shall work and how they shall evaluate each other. Helping the trainee to reflectively review the context and the meaning of the therapeutic interaction, connecting his/her own reactions with the patient's activity and communications, can be considered the primary task of supervision.

References

Ekstein, R. & Wallerstein, R. (1958). *The Teaching and Learning of Psychotherapy*. New York: Basic Books.

Jacob, P. (1981). *The San Francisco project: the analyst at work*. In: R. Wallerstein (Ed.): *Becoming a Psychoanalyst. A Study of Psychoanalytic Supervision*. New York: International University Press, pp. 191–210.

Szecsödy, I. (1990). *The learning process in psychotherapy supervision*. Stockholm: Karolinska Institute, Academic Dissertation.

Szecsödy, I. (1994). Supervision—a complex tool for psychoanalytic training. *Scandinavian Psycho-analytic Review, 17*: 119–129.

Szecsödy, I. (1997). How is learning possible in supervision? In: B. Martindale, M. Mörner, E. Cid Rodrigues & J. P. Vidal (Eds.): *Supervision and its Vicissitudes*. London: Karnac, pp. 101–116.

Szecsödy, I. (2003). *Zur Dynamik der Interaktion in der Supervision*. PsA-Info *55*: 5–17. Berlin.

Szecsödy, I. (2008). Does anything go in psychoanalytic supervision? *Psychoanalytic Inquiry, 28*: 373–386.

Szecsödy, I. (2013a). Supervision should be a mutual learning experience. Reports and brief communications. *Scandinavian Psychoanalytic Review, 36*(2): 126–129.

Szecsödy, I. (2013b). *Supervision and the Making of the Psychoanalyst*. IPI e-books. www.freepsychotherapybooks.com.

Tuckett, D. (2005). Does anything go? Towards a framework for the more transparent. *International Journal of Psychoanalysis, 86*: 31–49.

CHAPTER ONE

Theory of psychoanalytic psychotherapy supervision

Jill Savege Scharff

I became interested in the theory and practice of supervision when I noticed that mental health professionals were emerging from graduate school with inadequate preparation for psychoanalytic psychotherapy. Psychology programs emphasize diagnostic assessment and cognitive behavioral approaches; social work programs teach evidence-based treatment methods that are short-term and easily reimbursed by insurance companies; psychiatry trainees emerge with strong knowledge of pharmacological approaches to patient complaints, and so they are most likely to offer pharmacology consultation and medication review rather than arduous analytic psychotherapy which takes longer, feels emotionally demanding, and is less profitable. Those who find it more interesting to relate in depth to their patients quickly come up against their own limitations and need to seek continuing education. Theory and technique courses are important, but the most important thing is to get in to the room with the patient and do the work over time. To do that well the trainee psychotherapist requires clinical supervision.

Basic preparation for supervisors

What of the supervisors? What do they require? To be effective, they also need supervision. They need preparatory courses in the theory and technique of supervision; and they need a trusted group setting in which to develop their skills by listening to and discussing supervision experiences and challenges. Once a new supervisor is assigned a supervisee, she can present the challenges of that supervision in the group setting and learn how to be a good supervisor.

Just because a therapist has excellent clinical skills does not mean that she will be a good supervisor. Clinical skill is a prerequisite, and some of that skill and sensitivity is definitely useful in supervision. Certainly there is overlap in manner of listening, but supervision is quite distinct from therapy in aim. The task of supervision is facilitation and education, not healing. The task is also evaluative and prescriptive. Supervisors need to be aware of the complications arising from the duality of the facilitating and evaluative aspects of the supervisory role, each being essential to the learning process. When the evaluation process is organized as a two-way process with freely flowing input from the trainee, the supervisor can learn how best to meet the trainee's learning style.

Much of what I will describe of the role of the supervisor applies whether the supervision occurs in a private setting or in an institution. But the setting for supervision does introduce specific variables that need to be taken into account. In the institutional context the role of supervisor is complicated by other institutional positions held. For instance, a supervisee may feel privileged to be assigned to a supervisor who is the director of his training program, but, cowed by the weight of that authority, may inhibit his evaluative feedback for fear of retaliation that could affect his progress, graduation, or promotion within the institution. Keeping this transference aspect and possible conflict of interest in mind, the supervisor needs to give careful attention to role and boundary. In the private setting, supervision may be a choice not a requirement. It may take the form of consultation rather than supervision. This feels much more collegial. But the supervisor must bear in mind that she still shares legal responsibility for the care of the patient, and so there is always an evaluative aspect even when it is not as obvious as when a report of progress must be made to a training authority. Whether in privately arranged or programmatically required supervision, the relationship between supervisor and supervisee will reflect the relationship between the supervisee and his patient. There is some disagreement as to how to work with this inevitable resonance, as I will discuss later in this chapter.

The aim of clinical supervision is to teach psychotherapy. How do we do that? We establish a secure setting with a reliable frame within which we teach first and foremost a language for communicating experience. Within the frame, supervisee and supervisor engage in an emotional human interaction with a fine balance of support and confrontation, as supervisee and patient do during therapy. As we listen to clinical material we connect it to concepts of theory and technique. We help the supervisee to develop a way of working with the patient under discussion, and this practical knowledge transfers as a way of thinking about clinical situations in general.

The frame and focus of supervision

Supervision occurs within a frame, just as therapy does, and we maintain that frame as a secure, well-bounded environment within which to work. The frame has been described by Szecsödy (1997) as having stationary, mobile, and focused aspects.

The *stationary* aspect of the frame refers to the contract to meet at a certain regular time and place at a particular fee to be paid by a certain date, to discuss one individual, couple or family in depth, and to use an agreed method of reporting. Supervisors vary in how they accept clinical material. Some like to listen to the supervisee's narrative, some ask for discussions of problems encountered, others require full process notes. I prefer full process notes of at least one session, and if the supervision has to be on the telephone or Skype, I ask for written notes so that I can follow more easily. This is especially important if the remote supervisee is not fluent in English. The added value of process notes in giving access to the detail of the session, the back and forth between supervisor and supervisee, makes the extra effort worthwhile for the supervisee. Some supervisors work with audiotapes of sessions for more accurate recall, and that has its uses, especially in research, but that would not be my choice. I do not want tape-recording of sessions, because I want to work with not what actually happened but with what is filtered through the mind and memory of the therapist in training.

The *mobile* aspect of the frame refers to supervisor and supervisee maintaining a continuous reflection on their way of working in supervision. Some supervisors do include the supervisee's style as a subject for inquiry, or more accurately they focus on her characterological problems shown in relating to the supervisory task. They notice if she is passive or aggressive, intellectualizing or too empathic with her patients, submissive or omniscient in relation to the supervisor. They focus on tendencies to have poor boundaries, to be poorly prepared, or to present the material in a confusing way, so as to help the supervisee mature as a supervisee, with the expectation that this corrective will carry-over into her way of managing therapy and communicating with her patient.

The *focus* aspect of the frame refers to attention being given to the interaction of patient and therapist and the interaction of the supervisor and supervisee. We can distinguish three types of focus in supervision: Some supervisors use a didactic, patient-centered approach, that is to say, they focus solely on the patient/therapist dyad and do not address the supervisee/supervisor relationship (Tarachov, 1963). These supervisors emphasize the instructional aspect of supervision and steer well clear of any slippage into therapy territory. They teach the theory of the therapeutic relationship. They regard transference to the supervisor as a problem split off from the transference to the analyst, and they see countertransference as evidence of unanalyzed neurotic conflict. They do not address these manifestations but refer them back to the supervisees' personal or training analysis.

Other supervisors use an object relations approach. They focus less on the content of the clinical case presentation and more on the process of object relations found in the patient/therapist/supervisor relationship triangle and in the complex network of transferences and countertransferences occurring there. Through attending to these realities, the supervisor hopes to facilitate a transformation in the supervisee's self-awareness and clinical acumen. The focus here is not on what the supervisee should do, but on what he did do and how it was received by his patient in therapy and by the supervisor in supervision, and on how he receives the supervisor's comments. The supervisor attends closely to the supervisor/supervisee interaction, exploring slips and silences, as together they review the impact of the interventions. The aim is to express a psychoanalytic orientation towards the conduct and process of supervision, without psychoanalyzing the supervisee.

In summary, the supervisor may focus on one person, either the patient or the supervisee. She may focus on two people in interaction, the patient/therapist or the supervisee/supervisor. She may focus on multiple person interaction, patient or supervisee, patient/therapist, supervisee/supervisor. In my view, the multiple interactional focus is preferable, and will include attention to institutional influences and constraints on the therapist's work and on the supervisory process.

Whichever focus supervisors espouse, they face a loyalty conflict over their concern for the patient's needs or for the supervisee's growth. They may want to focus on the supervisee's learning difficulties but instead find themselves becoming preoccupied with the patient's dynamics, or the supervisee's unanalyzed conflicts. They may be so sensitive to the supervisees' unconsciously determined affects, perceptions, and behaviors that they feel pulled in to offer interpretation as if they were analysts, not supervisors. If a supervisor comes to believe that her supervisee's analyst is ineffectual she may attempt to rescue the situation by making a recommendation for a new analyst. Better to invite the supervisees to explore their blind spots further in their own analysis.

Facing role conflict

Supervisors also face conflict with their supervisees. Because the supervisor often also has an evaluative role, and at the very least brings with her the authority of years of clinical experience, there is a power differential that can bring out resistances and problems with authority. The unscrupulous or inadequately prepared supervisor may abuse that power by lording it over the supervisee, judging his competence against unrealistic standards, reporting harshly on progress, and giving in to prejudice and discrimination against him. The supervisee may be reactively argumentative or unduly compliant. The good supervisor considers this, not as evidence of neurotic conflict or pathology (which it may partly be) but as a sign of difficulty learning within this supervisory context. Monitoring the relationship, maintaining an open dialogue, prevents unfairness to the supervisee and provides a vehicle for reparation when problems have occurred.

Transference and countertransference come into focus in the supervisee's clinical interaction with her patient but they also color the supervisor's feelings about the supervisee and vice versa, as transferences to figures in early life are stimulated in therapeutic and supervisory relationships, both of which are characterized by a power differential like that in the parent/child relationship. In addition, the supervisor has feelings about the supervisee in reaction to both the supervisee's defenses against learning and the supervisor's anxieties about being an effective teacher.

Learning difficulties in the supervisee occur because of a fear of being exposed and then being found insufficient. The supervisee is afraid of feeling small, being embarrassed by the clinical material, or ashamed of her work with it. She does not want to feel anxious about her work and is terrified of seeming insane as she grapples with her patient's primitive anxieties. Teaching difficulties occur when the supervisor is afraid of losing authority because of not knowing enough. Then she pretends to know when she does not, and defends against this by becoming competitive with her supervisee, or using jargon to give a false sense of confidence and an air of belonging to the analytic world. Instead of saying such things as, "Tell me more. How did you feel? Did any fantasy cross your mind at that moment?" The insecure supervisor ties up her anxiety in a technical comment full of jargon that closes the space for thinking and splits off the necessary recall of whichever emotion had accompanied the clinical moments being presented. The supervisor may lack awareness of having her own weak, blind and dumb spots. She may be too dependent on the approval of the supervisee. She may mince her words because of being afraid that speaking directly will hurt her supervisee or make her angry. Then she may fear being displaced when the supervisee who is not satisfied asks to transfer to another supervisor.

Tasks of supervision

The first task of the supervisor is to create a secure base for learning. He comes well prepared from his own years of clinical experience, seminars in supervisory technique, and supervision of his supervision when he was beginning his appointment as a supervisor. He provides clear boundaries, a clear focus, and an egalitarian, friendly and safe holding environment for the supervisee and thereby for the patient/therapist couple. Having created the context, he and the supervisee are ready to interact with challenging clinical material. He absorbs anxieties and metabolizes them, giving them back to the supervisee in thinkable, manageable form. With an enquiring attitude, and no need of jargon and no jumping to premature conclusions, he opens a transitional space in which meaning can emerge from experience and reflection. He faces gaps in his knowledge without shame. He tolerates criticism and learns from it. He remains open to learning and self-examination, and so provides a model for identification as an ethical analyst in a state of life-long learning.

The supervisor is responsible for imparting an ethical stance. He ensures that the supervisee understands that her ethical duty is to her patient, to her profession, and to society. He speaks of the need to ensure informed consent for the proposed treatment to be supervised and to inform the patient of the background presence of the supervisor. It is the supervisor's duty to ensure the supervisee's competence and commitment to observe confidentiality of the patient's identity, clinical material, and records, and to fight to maintain the privilege in any court proceedings. In light of this, the supervisor asks the supervisee to disguise the identity of her patient when presenting to him or to a case conference and when writing up the case for a journal. The supervisor raises objection to any hint of exploitation of the patient that occurs to gratify the therapist's sexual, social, or financial desires, and similarly does not engage himself with the supervisee in exploitative ways.

Features of good and bad supervision

The qualities that make for a good supervisor have been studied by De la Torre and Applebaum (1974). They found that the good supervisor has tact, sensitive timing of interventions, empathy for the patient and the supervisee, and intuitive ability. She shows respect for her supervisee's work, courage in taking on challenges, and frankness in confronting difficulties (her own as well as those of her supervisee). She works with an attitude of inquiry and reflectiveness, open-ness to personal associations, adaptability, and mutuality. In role as a teacher, she is nevertheless a learner alongside her supervisee. In a study of psychotherapy supervision, Thomas (2004) found that clinical social work trainees most valued a good working alliance and an attitude of mutuality and respect (and see Chapter Seven). They were against any exploitation of the power differential. They preferred a supervisor of integrity, one who attends to the supervisee's concerns and treats her in a personal, optimally responsive manner, and whose perceptions they could trust. They wanted to be sure of supervisors' interest in their experience.

According to the clinical social workers interviewed for the study, the good supervisor inquires deeply into the clinical material and the supervisee's experience of it, encourages a rich description, and evokes a sense of being with the patient. She provides a holding, containing, transformative experience. She is empathic, stays attuned, focuses on the therapist's narrative, and tracks affectively charged concerns. She engages willingly in an open analysis of what may have gone wrong between therapist and patient, and between supervisee and supervisor. The interviewees added that they prefer a supervisor who does not charge for missed sessions! I myself do not charge for missed sessions because I am not the analyst and do not have the authority to investigate the unconscious meaning of the lapse, nor do I want that to become a focus. By not holding the supervisee personally accountable I feel free to investigate how the cancellation relates to the patient–therapist or supervisee–supervisor dynamics in relation to the patient's dynamics.

Thomas's interviewees also identified aspects of bad supervision. They pointed to supervisors who engaged in power struggles and dual relationships on the one hand and a lack of collegiality on the other. The bad supervisor does not inspire trust and inhibits learning by being intimidating and pouncing on the supervisee. They did not appreciate supervisors who were too neutral and abstinent and who charged for missed sessions as if the supervisee were in analysis. They described bad supervisors whom they experienced variously as critical, judgmental, disparaging, condescending, controlling, and frustrating of the supervisee and disrespectful of the client. Some bad supervisors were unreliable and procrastinating. The worst of the lot were indiscreet, unethical, and careless of boundaries.

Similarities and differences in supervision and analysis

When the supervisor brings analytic sensibility to the supervision, boundaries are essential to ensure that supervision stays on task and does not get conflated with psychoanalysis. Supervision is not analysis. Analysis is open-ended without goals. Supervision is goal oriented and time limited. The analyst listens with suspended attention, dealing with the patient's unconscious fantasy and the historical roots of conflict. The supervisor listens with selective attention, choosing learning problems to focus on. The supervisor is oriented to the reality of the supervisee's clinical work in the present, not to unconscious fantasy and infantile conflict. The aim of analysis is to reach a deep understanding of the analysand's unconscious. The aim of supervision is deep understanding of the unconscious process of the patient, not of the supervisee. From time to time, the supervisor or supervisee may identify with the patient and the supervisor may identify with the supervisee because, transference and countertransference do occur in supervision. The transference may be idealizing in nature (especially if the supervisor is highly empathic to the supervisee's vulnerability) denigratory (when one of the pair seems incompetent), or persecutory (when the supervisor, not the patient, is seen as the source of the supervisees' discomfort). Rather than fall into the trap of analyzing the transference, the supervisor looks at the influence on the dynamics of the patient/therapist interaction on the supervisory relationship. The conflict that the supervisory dyad has experienced can be used to learn about the patient by illuminating the patient/therapist interaction. This can, of course, be used defensively to avoid dealing with conflict that truly does emanate from the supervisory dyad. As I said earlier, keeping up an open dialogue maintains a safe, clear space that can reflect the patient/therapist dynamics without distortion by intrusion originating instead from supervisor/supervisee dynamics. Open communication is the best antidote to disruptive conflict clouding the supervisory relationship.

The phenomenon of conflict in the supervisory relationship mirroring conflict in the patient–therapist relationship has been named parallel process. But it seems a misnomer, because at these times the therapy process does not in fact remain in parallel to the supervision at all. On the contrary, the therapy process explodes within the supervision, as the supervisee imports the patient interaction. Resonance seems a preferable term. Another way to put it is to think of supervision as a fractal of the therapeutic encounter. Supervision has a similar pattern to therapy but on a smaller scale. In their interaction in supervision, supervisee and supervisor create a dynamic footprint of the therapy session being reported. Their interaction carries clues to the transference/countertransference dialectic. Then the supervisee imports the learning from supervision back into the therapy (Scharff & Scharff, 2000).

The point has been made in various ways that an open dialogue in a secure relationship is essential to supervision that is effective. Open communication all along prepares the secure base from which the supervisor proceeds to produce a report on the supervisee's progress. In a one-way supervision model, the supervisor simply writes a paragraph of impressions. In a mutual supervisory process, supervisor and supervisee write their impressions of each other and discuss them. Unfortunately supervisors' reports are too often focused on the patient's progress, not the supervisee's movement along the learning curve. The usefulness of this information can be somewhat improved by referring to a standardized checklist that attends to specific measures of growth and makes an inventory of weak, dumb and blind spots that interfere with learning. A thorough report focuses on the supervisee's learning difficulties and areas for growth. It addresses conflict and role ambiguity when the supervisory dyad is embedded in an institution in which each of them has other roles and relationships in the teaching and learning environment. The complete report also reflects on the supervisory relationship as well. But the supervisor cannot write about that, or anything else, without access to the supervisee's impressions of his style and capacity to listen and communicate knowledge. In short, it has to be a shared evaluation process, and it is most effective when done openly, mutually, and continuously, and not only when a report is due (Scharff & Scharff, 2000; Varela & J. Scharff, 1999).

In summary, like therapy, effective supervision depends on the quality of the relationship between supervisor and supervisee. Learning difficulty is to be expected and is not a sign of pathology. Teaching difficulties are to be expected and worked out in dialogue with the supervisee, in the supervisor's own individual supervision, and in a supervision discussion group. Conflict is to be expected and negotiated openly. Evaluation must be mutual if supervision is to be most effective. Good supervision is transformative for the supervisee, and thereby for the patient.

References

De la Torre, J. & Applebaum, A. (1994). Use and misuse of clichés in clinical supervision. *Archives of General Psychiatry, 31*(3): 302–306.

Shanfield, S. B., Hetherly, V. V., & Matthews, K. L. (2001). Excellent supervision: the residents' perspective. *Journal of Psychotherapy Practice and Research, 10*(1): 23–27.

Shanfield, S. B., Matthews, K. L., & Hetherly, V. V. (1993). What do excellent psychotherapy supervisors do? *American Journal of Psychiatry, 150*(7): 1081–1084.

Scharff, J. & Scharff, D. (2000). *Tuning the Therapeutic Instrument.* Northvale, NJ: Jason Aronson.

Szecsödy, I. (1997). How is learning possible in supervision? In: *Supervision and its Vicissitudes*, ed. B. Martindale, M. Mörner, C. Rodriguez, and J. P. Vidal, pp. 101–116. London: Karnac.

Tarachov, S. (1963). *An Introduction to Psychotherapy.* New York: IUP.

Teitebaum, S. H. (1990). Supertransference: the role of the supervisor´s blind spots. *Psycho-analysis and Psychology, 7*(2): 243–258, 1990.

Thomas, E. (2004). "A Study of Supervisory Experience." PhD thesis. Social Work Institute, Washington DC.

Varela, Y. de G. de P. & Scharff, J. S. (1999). A supervisor/supervisee evaluation design. International Psychotherapy Institute, www. theipi.org. Chevy Chase Maryland.

CHAPTER TWO

Boundaries in supervision

Jaedene Levy

Supervision and therapy are similar in that both modalities involve a helper and one who wants help. Both are interpersonal helping processes working with the same affective components. Many of the elements of supervision are also found in therapy. These are:

1. The affective relationship
2. The wish to change, opposed by the resistance to change
3. The struggle against being dependent
4. The unconscious, repetitive way of taking hold of a problem
5. The attempt to master a new experience
6. The linking of past helping experiences with the present experience.

The supervisor's opening question in a supervisory hour, "What do you want to discuss?" isn't too different from the therapist's approach to a patient. So how do supervisors ensure that the supervisory process is not a hidden form of therapy? Good supervisors and therapists are clear that they are distinguished by their differences in purpose.

While a therapist may occasionally help a patient with practical matters, and a supervisee may benefit personally from a supervisory comment, these gains are secondary to the main purpose. With patients, the defining factor is the resolution of the inner conflict, a therapeutic purpose. With supervisees, it's the achievement of greater skill in work with patients, an educational purpose.

Along with the difference in purpose is the manner in which therapist and supervisee work to define their goals with their patients and supervisees respectively. In psychotherapy, patients, in essence, set their own goals in collaboration with their therapist. And these goals may change as the process develops and makes for change.

In supervision, the clinical program or professional discipline, whose representative is the supervisor, sets its requirements and goals in terms of standards of professional ethics, work performance, and clinical treatment. Thus the supervision furnishes the external yardstick to which both supervisor and supervisee must measure up. The supervisor and supervisee agree to this contract.

The supervisor has a body of knowledge to convey through the supervisory process. The supervisee states her desire to acquire this body of knowledge. The idea is that the supervisee will become a better therapist by receiving this instruction. Not only that, the supervisee is a professional colleague who may eventually do what the supervisor is doing. Herein lies a major difference between teaching and treating patients.

Supervision begins with establishing the frame of treatment and the boundaries of supervision. There must be a basic frame for supervisor and supervisee to count on, just as there is between therapist and patient. As the training continues, both supervisor and supervisee will feel increasingly secure within it. This enhanced security will lead to greater honesty with one another.

The frame consists of the boundaries and agreed upon conditions under which the supervision will take place. It involves defining the day and time of supervision, the frequency of sessions, the length of each supervision session, fees, and cancellation policies. The supervisee describes the intended focus of the supervision, and the supervisor assents or finds a mutually agreeable alternative focus that meets the needs of the supervisee and any program requirements that apply. The supervisor explains how the material is to be presented, usually requiring process recordings. Supervisor and supervisee agree to the need for evaluations and discuss when these will be done and with whom they will be shared. Once these conditions are set, the supervisor and the supervisee have made a commitment to an agreed upon acceptable framework in which to work. The frame should remain flexible, however, to suit changing needs and goals. The frame may be modified by mutual agreement of supervisor and supervisee.

Within that frame, supervisors enable their supervisees to develop a dialogue about the affective experiences in doing the therapy. This eventually equips supervisees to identify, contain, and analyze affective experiences on their own. The educational goal is for supervisees to acquire facility with self reflection and self analysis. As supervisees learn to contain, identify, and analyze a given emotion in themselves, they are able to tolerate and integrate their own affective resonances in the treatment—and in the supervision too.

A supervision challenge

Pamela, an attractive, energetic person, had been in practice as a psychotherapist for several years when she came to me for supervision. She said that she chose me because she felt that I had knowledge, ability, and, most important to her, "her kind of personality." The case she wished to discuss was that of a husband and a wife, whom she had originally seen as a couple, but had decided to treat individually.

Pamela's narrative of the therapeutic process was frequently interrupted by her telling me of unhappy excerpts about her own marriage, and repeating statements of advice she had offered to each of her patients. I felt drawn to her lively personality, and pulled in to thinking about her revelations concerning her personal life. But, I felt uncomfortable about being used in this way.

Pamela felt that the clinical problem she faced was being able to stop herself from telling each spouse about the other's intimate details shared with her in their individual therapies. When I voiced my concerns about the compromised status of treating both spouses at the same time, she became defensive. She told me that I was too inflexible in my thinking and supervising.

Pamela didn't want to write process recordings, she simply wanted to tell me about her patients. I felt that I didn't know what she was doing with them. I couldn't get a clear picture. Sitting with her, I felt confused and anxious because the boundaries in our professional relationship were being blurred by her refusal to report methodically and by her narrative being interspersed with revelations about her marriage, just as she felt anxious about revealing information between spouses. The problem in the therapy was re-created in the supervision, but without a basis from which to use my understanding of the parallel process for the benefit of Pamela and her patients. So, the problems between us began to obscure the problems she was experiencing in the therapy with her patients.

Finally Pamela told me that what she really wanted was to be my friend. I explained that that would not be possible during the supervision, because we needed to maintain the supervisory framework, just as in therapy, one needs to maintain the frame. She told me that she had been friendly with her former supervisor throughout that supervision. She said that in contrast, I was rigid and narrow minded, unable to support her kind of work. I made her too unhappy and anxious about her work.

Pamela decided that she needed to find a supervisor who would be comfortable with blurred boundaries, and would accept her way of working. She used a highly emotive image to convey to me how I had failed her. She said that she preferred a supervisor with leaky breasts, and I was not that. Indeed, I do not think of myself that way.

I knew that Pamela wasn't able to hear me or feel the support that I did have to offer. I felt both relieved and guilty when she left. I would have liked to get to a place where I could function in ways that she could learn from, but I did not want to be a "leaky breast." Reflecting on this, I came to feel that I had drawn the lines with her prematurely and too rigidly, because I felt so anxious about not really knowing or understanding what she was doing with her patients. I feel that I should have explored more fully what she felt was problematic for her, rather than responding to what was problematic for me. I think she became frightened, as I did, and that blocked her thinking and exploration with me.

The more inexperienced the supervisees are, the greater their tendency to infuse their clinical work with subjective distortions which then present as difficulties that inhibit learning from the supervisor. Unresolved issues stirred up in the relationship with the supervisor may lead to automatic, inappropriate responses from the supervisee to the patient and to the supervisor as well.

The good supervisor will insist on certain basic rules, but will leave sufficient leeway for supervisor and supervisee to their own unique adaptation based on their individual skills and relational dynamic. There should be freedom to be individuals, but respect for each other's views, for the process, and the relationship.

When supervisees do not have process notes ready on time or do not bring them at all, or on the other hand present an obsessive, overly complete collection of data, they tend to avoid the elements that comprise the emotional climate and ignore the true inner affective and cognitive responses to their patients' material as well.

There is no absolute as to what is a perfect process recording. Perfection cannot be imposed on supervisees anyway. What is ideal in each instance depends on the supervisees' ability to recall, report accurately, communicate the feeling tone of their sessions, and supervisors' capacity to listen and reflect. All psychotherapists have their own style of communication with their patients, and it varies from one patient to another, depending on the unique communication skills of each patient.

We need to mobilize the processes that facilitate learning and to determine what difficulties limit it. This requires introspection, willingness to change, and a capacity to grow. But "change" has a different meaning in supervision than it does in therapy. With patients, the decision to seek therapy is an acknowledgement of some problem or dissatisfaction in their personal life. With supervisees, the decision to seek supervision reflects their willingness to offer their work up to joint scrutiny, not their whole self, but the part of them that relates to professional learning. The change therefore, is limited to one area, but within that one area, the change may still be far reaching and deep, because it involves allowing oneself to be vulnerable and open to criticism.

The supervisor's task is a delicate one. Dealing with the inner life of the supervisee calls for tact and forbearance while fostering affective expression in appropriate ways. The supervisor gradually develops comfort in moving back and forth between more and less affective modes of expression. The litmus test of appropriateness in degree of self revelation by the supervisee in supervision is relevance. Will the self revelation relate to or interfere with the basic goals of supervision? The supervisor monitors the degree to which self revelation contributes meaningfully to the therapy of the patient and to the education of the supervisee.

A discussion of private material could have a proper place if it improves the clinical work and is for the good of the patient. It has no place if the supervisee becomes the patient. Often there's uncertainty about where the limits should be, especially at the beginning of a supervisory relationship, because the supervisor doesn't know much about the supervisee. Therefore the comfort zone should be explored collaboratively. Having embarked on self revelation, they need not continue it for longer than seems educationally useful.

Dealing with overidentification

Ellen is working towards her final licensure. She has been out of social work school for one year. She works at a clinic with some very difficult patients. She had chosen to discuss in supervision a young woman in her early 20's who has an eating disorder, cuts herself, and periodically hints at considering suicide.

Ellen explained that she was unable to write a real process recording because her sessions ended late in the evening, and she was too tired. I asked her to tell me more. She said, "I just don't want to do them. I don't want to go to that level of pain. When I write, I can feel more than when I'm sitting in the session. I'm in therapy and working on myself, but for now, I just want to tell you that feeling so intensely after the session is why I want to simply tell you about the patient, and decide what to do. In the real world, out there, you can't just let someone leave if they're mentioning cutting. I do casework in my real job and I just need to have a plan with this woman."

The problem here is that the supervisee is resonating with her patient's pain, rather than subjecting it to process and review. The supervisor, vested with the authority of knowledge and accreditation, must insist on full clinical reports, whether written or verbal, sufficient to convey the process. Recording the process is an effective way to establish the boundary between helper and help-seeker.

The supervisor worked with Ellen to establish the distinction between her role as therapist and the patient's experience. The supervisor explained that to be helpful, the therapist must be empathic and yet present an objective view of reality that the patient can come to grips with in the course of the therapeutic process. Confronting difficulty doesn't mean assaulting the integrity of the supervisee. It just means maintaining a separate, reflective stance. The supervisor must be able to indicate the distinction between the supervisor and the supervisee in order for the business of professional learning to be accomplished.

The relationship that the supervisor has with the supervisee gets reflected in the work of the supervisee with the patient. We might think of how a couple's relationship affects their child so as to consider the question of boundaries through that lens. When parents don't provide boundaries, children become scared, and often react by being out of control. There is little for them to hold on to or hit up against. If they do not get an indicator of when to stop and when to go, they do not get a sense of where one begins and ends. Parents may feel guilty about setting boundaries, and when they do, children may resent them but that is how they learn the rules and how things work. Other parents apply rigid rules and set inflexible boundaries. Inflexibility creates a different set of problems. When parents can't be responsive to changing needs, the child may feel like a mere object, not recognized as an individual.

By analogy, the supervisor is like a good parental couple setting firm limits and relating well to the needs of the young person. The basis of supervision is setting good, firm boundaries, holding consistently to an educational stance, and permitting freedom of affective expression within those clearly delineated parameters, and at the same time, being flexible enough to allow the supervisee's individuality to determine the shape of the supervisory process. Under these conditions, supervisor and supervisee have a unique, authentic experience in which to learn from one another. And the quality of this relationship carries forward as a well informed, seasoned professional therapeutic attitude in the supervisee's work with patients.

CHAPTER THREE

Supervision as a model of containment for a turbulent patient

Mary Jo Pisano

In clinical supervision, supervisor and supervisee/therapist engage in a teaching/ learning relationship with an established explicit contract, standard frame, agreed payment schedule, and accepted format for the case presentation. This parallels the therapist/patient relationship, and yet is quite different in that its goal is educational, not therapeutic. It is dedicated to the growth and development of the therapist. Bion said that becoming is a process which begins, continues, and is never completed. As parents we recognize, "However experienced we are, we still know very little indeed about how to bring up children, of whatever age. We are beginning to know that we do not know—that is something" (Bion, 1975, p. 147). As analytic therapists, we should always be in a state of becoming, whether we are in role as patients or therapists, supervisees or supervisors. I hope there will never be a time when psychotherapists cease from becoming or unwisely imagine they have arrived.

As a psychodynamic psychoanalytic therapist, I believe there are three important ingredients of meaningful and helpful therapy: First, the study of theory and technique, which enables the therapist to base treatment upon a solid philosophy of understanding; second, personal analysis or psychotherapy, which allows for ongoing self analysis for in-depth understanding of our patients; third, clinical supervision, which further facilitates our capacity to understand our patients and our own dynamics.

Clinical supervision is part of the very fabric of being a psychotherapist/psychoanalyst. Effective and useful clinical supervision is like a potent tincture: a little bit goes a long way. Supervision deeply affects the supervisee who in turn as a therapist affects a multitude of patients in ensuing years. The main goals of supervision are to provide knowledge, teach the necessary clinical skill, and develop the capacity to think. Developing the capacity to think clearly requires a containing relationship in which the supervisor listens, processes, reflects upon what he is told, and returns it to the supervisee in more manageable form. From this the supervisee can learn to contain her own thoughts and feelings, conscious and unconscious anxieties. It can be argued that a function of supervision is to metabolize the emotional turbulence arising in the interacting dynamics of the supervisory process—the dynamics of the therapist-patient and the supervisor–supervisee relationships.

The evolving supervisory relationship provides a holding and containing environment for the supervisee while she is learning to do the same for her patient. Winnicott (1963) believed that if a mother feels adequately held in her family to be the mother to her baby she will be more able to learn her baby's language and individual rhythms. She will learn from her baby how best to be the mother that baby needs her to be, each baby being different. She will find herself being a different mother to each of her babies. The baby benefits or suffers according to the quality of the support the mother receives from her partner or an extended family member. Similarly, the supervisor provides a form of holding for the therapist in supervision, which enables the therapist in turn to create a therapeutic alliance with her patient, makes it safe for her and her patient to become engaged in deep exploration, and facilitates the therapist's understanding and containment as she learns the language and rhythms of each patient.

Containment in supervision is a critical component of supervision. There will be times when therapist feelings spill over and project into the patient. Once this is recognized in supervision, the therapist can distinguish her self from her patient. The space created in supervision clarifies what is being communicated to the therapist consciously and unconsciously. The therapist can contemplate what is being projected, what is being introjected, what belongs to the therapist, and what belongs to the patient. Experiencing containment in supervision, the therapist can manage her feelings, gather her thoughts, and clear the path to engage in an understanding and thinking relationship with her patient. She is more able to empathize, create a therapeutic space, and clarify her perceptions of her patient. She then has the freedom to enter a state of reverie in which she can listen for associations, perceive multiple levels of meaning, and provide insight and interpretation.

Initially, the therapist/supervisee relies on the supervisor. The supervisee is careful about revealing her case material and may want to present mainly the good moments. Through thoughtful listening and reflection, the supervisor attends to what is being transferred to her, becoming aware of unconscious communications and her own countertransference experiences. In time, the supervisory input becomes integrated into the ongoing work with the patient. In learning to listen to her patients, the supervisee develops a deeper understanding of unconscious process. She increases her capacity for observing what is transpiring in the session, and comes to rely on her own voice, interpretations and conclusions. The supervisee develops a positive transference to supervisor, which allows an identification process to occur.

As the supervision process deepens, a trusting relationship is created, a safe environment is established. In this context, the supervisee learns how to think, develops her own style, compatible with her personality, and establishes an internal mechanism for observing and monitoring her work. Eventually, the therapist acquires her own capacity for reflection. She creates a space in her mind to observe herself. This does not signal the end of supervision, but marks the beginning of developing an aspect of her mind, an internal supervisor that is in dialogue with her supervisor (Casement, 1991).

Developing a containing relationship in supervision allows the supervisee to build the capacity not only to contain her own feelings but also to begin to understand dynamic interactions in the dyad. Looking beyond a narrow focus on the patient, she learns to examine the patient–therapist dyad, and beyond that to the supervisor and supervisee dyad, and so expands her capacity to understand internal object relationships and their expression in the external world. As her perspective enlarges, the therapist can appreciate how affect and relationship affect thinking. This learning from the workings of the supervisory dyad is further reinforced when the therapist attends an affective group that gathers to study analytic concepts and sees them inevitably enacted by unconscious transmission in the sub-groups that form in response (Scharff & Scharff, 2000).

In our clinical practice, we encounter cases that test our capacity to think, blur our vision of what is happening, interfere with our facility for interpretation, and in general bewilder us. We lose our direction, like an explorer without a compass, not knowing how to proceed. Some therapists struggle privately and others seek direction from a senior, more knowledgeable clinician. I will now give an example from the supervision that convinced me of the value of supervision for even an experienced clinician.

Example from a supervisee

My supervisor and I began our journey of thinking, reflecting, and processing my experience with a challenging, turbulent patient, John, who exhibited symptoms that fit the features of schizophrenia. As therapy intensified, John revealed that he felt conspired against, spied upon, and possibly drugged by a friend. He reported feelings of intense anxiety, depression, anger, sleep disturbance, sexual identity concerns, and obsessive compulsive behavior. He said, "I am crazy. I am schizophrenic. I am multiple." This could fit neatly into differential diagnosis of a young person with major mood disorder, major mental illness, maybe psychosis.

I had many questions. How frequently should he be seen in psychotherapy? Does he need medication? Would he hurt himself or someone else? Is he engaged in substance abuse (drugs and/or alcohol)? Is he struggling with sexual identity concerns? Is he exhibiting signs of schizophrenia? I did not want to travel down the path of focusing on symptoms only. I wanted to figure out what the symptoms were telling me about John's fears, his guilt, his shame, his anger, his hope, his desire, and his internal world.

Attending to his major symptoms, without losing track of the total situation and the total person, was difficult. It required me to contain much anxiety in order to continue to think. I believed that an experienced clinician would assist me in containing my anxiety, avoid getting involved in any enactments, and gain greater insight into John's dynamics. Understanding the dynamics of his internal world and the meaning of his symptoms would be such a challenge that I wanted and needed someone experienced to think with me.

The patient

John, a 19-year-old college student, majoring in anthropology, made a contract with me for twice-a-week psychotherapy. He had had directive behavioral counseling at University already. He said, "I liked that therapy because I like people telling me what to do, even though I don't put it into practice." He laughed at this. In our initial sessions, he tried to get me to tell him what to do, as if wanting to remain a child.

John, a smooth freckled faced, bright blonde Caucasian man appeared younger than his age. He had had a late pubescence, his voice remaining high-pitched until junior year of high school, a fact he tried to hide by faking a deep voice. He is still upset with himself about not being himself. Yet, he is afraid to be who he is.

John is the second of four boys, with a brother two years older and twins two years younger. John's father had been a Christian missionary, but before marrying he had denounced his faith and became estranged from his family. John knows very little about his father's family history except that depression runs in the family and that one of his Father's cousins killed himself. John describes his father as "a humble, quiet, alpha dog who stands on the periphery at a party." Having found his father's high school year book in the basement, and paging through it, he discovered that his father had been a star athlete, a fact that neither he nor his mother had been told.

John describes his mother as a woman who has an "anxiety disorder", had an "eating disorder until she was 30", and who "simply talks too much". She is indeed anxious, has phobias, and avoids crossing bridges. She has worried most of her life about her mentally ill sister, who in her freshman year of college had a severe mental breakdown described as either "manic-depressive or schizophrenic." Like this aunt, John is a second child and he is finishing his freshman year.

John describes his older brother as a "very fidgety" man with some distorted thoughts and a drinking problem. On a visit home, John heard this brother say, "My mother doesn't seem like my mother." John worries about his two younger brothers who are shy and fearful. He worries they will develop a mental illness. Actually he wishes that his whole family would be in treatment. "They could benefit from family therapy," he said.

John elaborated on his complaints: "I am worried about my future. I might faint. I am stressed. I might change and become somebody else.

I am angry with friends, especially my female friends. I am afraid people will not like me. I get more attention from my mother than my brothers. I have thoughts that worry me. I have a problem with people pleasing. I even laugh at jokes that aren't funny, agreeing when I don't agree. I try to get everything right. I don't express my anger. I am afraid of failure. I am trying to find my own style. I fear criticism. I am afraid I will become mentally ill; no matter how I try to avoid it, like Eliot Smith, that musician who killed himself."

Excerpts from sessions

John said, "If I am myself, I will say or do something to hurt somebody. I keep to myself, so I don't damage anyone. I am always trying to do the right thing, live the right way. My mother bothers me. The way she dresses, the way she wears her scarf, cheap coats, the way she wears her hair. (He showed me a picture of her on his cell phone). I don't like the way she talks. She is always stressed. She claims everyone blames her. She cries! I don't feel like I am myself. I am afraid I am a part of her. It is strange that she is my Mom."

John relayed a story about his brother teasing him and saying that their mother didn't love him. John ran into the forest. He continued, "I wanted them to come after me, and they did. I wanted my brother to feel bad. I felt rage and wanted to retaliate. My mother never helped me!"

John talked about a story he had written concerning a group of men desiring the same woman. I thought of brothers fighting for their mother's attention.

"I day dream, I zone out, light headiness. I am afraid I will get out of control and dissociate. My aunt, who is mentally ill, had a seizure at a family picnic. The thought of being crazy frightens me."

"A friend gave me a drink. I wouldn't drink it. Maybe he put something in it. I forced the thought out of my head. I am paranoid!"

Over the next weeks, we explored more of his aggressive, angry feelings. As we did this, he began to organize his thoughts. Then, unexpectedly, he wanted to be hospitalized. He tried to reach me on my cell phone, which I use for emergencies but he dialed the wrong number. A little girl's voice answered. He was so angry with me that he thought he might hurt this little girl, who he imagined might be my daughter. He was fearful that I might hurt him.

In the following sessions, he increased his investment in being mentally ill:

> "I am afraid I am schizophrenic or maybe MPD. What if I stop worrying, maybe, I would think I could be a prophet. I remember when I was a senior in high school looking in the mirror and thinking I am as beautiful as Jesus. A friend told me about a guy who thought he was Jesus and drove a car in a tree and killed himself. He was a skate boarder. (John is a skate boarder). Suicide crosses my mind. Everything is piling up. I can't sleep. I am having memory loss and feelings of unreality."
>
> "When I came here today, I saw a statue in someone's yard. Maybe it is a robot that could spy on us. I thought I heard someone whispering my name. Last year in the dorm, there was red light over the bed. I thought it was a camera and someone was watching me. (One Flew over the Cuckoo's Nest). All is getting blurred. I can't remember how I used to be. Many fears dominate me. I am stressed. Maybe I need medication?"

Turning point in the treatment

At this point, we addressed our relationship and the relationship with his mother:

> "I am so angry with my Mom for not raising me better. There is so much anxiety in my family. I am so fearful and anxious, today."

He began to explore his anger towards his mother; afraid he is too similar to her. He began to confront his anger with me too. More in touch with our relationship, he was fearful of expressing thoughts that might disturb me.

> "I woke up today like a newborn. Then, it set in—the feeling of unreality and tension in my head. I went to a lecture with Julia Serrano. She was born a man and became a woman. There was a war going on inside her. I am thinking of old videos in my head where I look gay and girlie. I have homosexual feelings from time to time and worry I will become gay. It is upsetting."

I inquired about his internal war but he went back to the lecture by Julia Serrano. "She said, 'Do all that you want to do as long as you aren't mean.' She gave us a flyer. It scared me. I tore it up when I got home. I thought it had some power."

> "I might say something that upsets you. I remember when I was a freshman in high school, thinking I was gay, I felt attracted to my best friend and wanted to kiss him. I prayed to God not to be gay. I admire gay men's style. I was angry with my friend, who is dominant. He said, 'You are a communist.' And I smiled foolishly and wanted to harm him. I am afraid I would say I want to kill someone."

I had lots of questions, many concerns, and much anxiety. Was my patient schizophrenic? In private practice, I treat many severely abused patients and major disorders, but this young man' disturbing thoughts and feelings did not fit a clear diagnosis. His thinking was distorted and he exhibited a great deal of paranoia. I was considering a referral for medication, because I was very concerned about his depression and his anxiety. I did an assessment of his drug and alcohol use to determine if that contributed to his hysterical, paranoid, anxious and depressed state of mind. I was very aware of his immaturity both physically and emotionally, and yet he had chosen a school 2500 miles from his hometown as if he wanted to establish more autonomy and independence. This decision gave me hope.

In supervision

Weekly, my supervisor and I discussed this case. My anxiety decreased as she functioned as a container. We thought about John, and we explored ideas together. Then I was able to function as a container for John to repair his early experience with a therapeutic relationship. I saw his "wild thoughts" creating intense anxious feelings and needing to have a thinker to manage them. I treated him as a person who wanted to behave like a crazy person, but wasn't crazy, who was underdeveloped and didn't want to grow up, and didn't want to deal with his sexual feelings, his anger, his fears and his dependent attachment to his mother, who, however, as he said, "couldn't help him."

Our work was collaborative, listening to each other and thinking together. As she contained me, we explored the following:

> I wanted to know where these "crazy thoughts" of his originated;
> how he was haunted by them; how thin-skinned he was, and how

easy it was for him to ingest other's thoughts. I continued to pursue his perception of reality, the meaning of his distorted thoughts, directing him to think in ordinary ways, and helping him transition from concrete to symbolic. I did this by posing questions to John: "Where did you get that idea? How did you arrive at thinking this? Where did you get these words?"

My supervisor encouraged me to pay attention to my countertransference, which was informative and communicative about his internal world and his positive and negative transferences to me. She taught me to listen to my anxiety and to understand that it was, at times, a projected identification with John's state of mind. Staying aware of the unconscious communication between us enabled me to track the development of our relationship. Our relationship was essential in helping John repair the developmental fissions and transfer his dependency to me, hoping that it would be a healthy and helping experience.

I increased my understanding of how John collapsed into concrete thinking when he is anxious. I encouraged him to see the symbolic meaning of his feelings and thoughts and to realize sometimes that his decisions are made on feelings while facts go missing. I held in mind that this was a very confused young man with intense feelings of anger, self betrayal, shame and guilt occurring under the umbrella of anxiety. By permitting him to articulate his thoughts about harming someone and harming himself, and attending to these thoughts seriously, I provided some calmness and helped him to decrease his fears. I continued to challenge him about trusting his own mind, holding on to his mind, and not losing his mind to mentally illness.

Unconsciously, John assumes that someone in his family needs to carry on the mental illness. We explored the burden of his being identified with his aunt. Perhaps to spare his brothers, he selected himself. Eventually he realized that he did not need to go crazy, his brothers did not have to be crazy either, and generational transmission can be extinguished. We examined his over-identification with his mother and how he introjected her worries. He realized that she was more equipped to handle her worries than he had thought.

If you met John today, he would appear as a typical 21-year-old, taking advantage of study abroad, and navigating the trip without parental interventions. He is focused on his academics and part-time employment. There is no evident paranoia and only a trace of anxiety. His thinking is organized, and he has moved through adolescent angst.

He has individuated and separated from his parents, particularly his mother. You would notice his caring about his girlfriend in the tone of his voice he uses to describe her and their relationship. Our present sessions are about ordinary developmental concerns: relationship issues, school issues, drugs, alcohol, cigarettes, and future life issues.

By having the opportunity to share my ideas freely in a collaborative, trusting and non-threatening environment with my supervisor, I was able to contain my anxiety and experience. I was held through the very difficult times of my patient's depression and his psychotic thinking and was able to understand and appreciate him through another lens.

In summary, I want to share something I read recently. Years ago, people believed that all swans were white, until a black swan was spotted in Australia (Taleb, 2010). One observation changed this belief forever. In the beginning of my exploration with John, his typical symptoms and the known diagnostic explanations would have led me to assess him as psychotic. As I deepened my understanding of him and his symptoms through supervision, I saw him as a young man with normal adolescent difficulties, absent psychosis. It was as if a black swan had been spotted. This tale speaks of the fragility of knowledge and the need to continue to think together, learn from experience, discover our patients anew, and develop ourselves as therapists.

References

Bion, W. R. (1975). *Brazilian lectures 2*. Rio de Janeiro: Imago Editora.

Bollas, C. (2002). *Free Association: Ideas in Psychoanalysis*. USA: Totem Books.

Casement, P. J. (1991). *Learning from Patients*. New York: Guildford Press.

Casement, P. J. (2002). *Learning from Our Mistakes*. New York: Guildford Press.

Scharff, J. S. & Scharff, D. E. (2000). *Tuning the Therapeutic Instrument*. Northvale NJ: Jason Aronson.

Slavin, J. H. (1997). Models of learning and psychoanalytic traditions: Can reform be sustained? *Psychoanalytic Dialogues, 7*: 803–817.

Taleb, N. N. (2010). *The Black Swan*. New York: Random House.

Winnicott, D. W. (1963). Dependence in infant-care, in child-care, and in the psychoanalytic setting. In: *The Maturational Processes and the Facilitating Environment*, pp. 249–259. New York: International Universities Press.

CHAPTER FOUR

Supervision or thera-vision? Working with unconscious motives in the supervisory encounter

Carl Bagnini

I want to discuss serious supervision difficulties in light of unconscious processes of projective identification that alter the frame in the triadic mental space of supervision (Bagnini, 2005). I view the supervision frame as a triadic phenomenological-affective field, various components of which foster clinical learning. These components are the supervisor's frame of reference for conducting the analytic task; his point of view concerning the need to create space for dialogue about the usefulness of his frame; and the supervisee/therapist's frame of reference for conducting treatment. The coming together of supervisor and supervisee's frames and personalities evokes emotional nuances that may impair learning by causing problematic regressive pulls, and may even render the supervisory frame useless. I will illustrate my discussion of supervision with a detailed study of a supervisee who subverted the supervisory frame because it conflicted with her personal preferences. I will show how her personality and learning style deeply challenged my supervisory abilities until I found a way to retrieve the frame and move forward.

One conclusion I have drawn from being supervised and supervising others is that some therapists are better prepared for case-focused learning then others. There are therapists who cannot grab hold of the essence of a listening position because they lack the ability to focus on unconscious derivatives of manifest material. Case discussions alone may not capture the thing trying to be said. The supervision experience is intended to be straightforward enough in that the conscious motives of supervisor and supervisee are ones of intention to collaborate. Consciously, supervisees urgently want help with clinical dilemmas. Unconsciously, they may experience the frame as a persecutory object. As they explore their daily work with patients, in-depth discussions bring out unconscious conflicts. Supervisees may provide rich clinical material for discussion and idealize the supervisor at first, but later they may remember less detail, become vague about what goes on in sessions, and generally provide incomplete process reports. (When I think about long term problems in supervision a book title comes to mind: "Things I never told my supervisor in supervision!") A critically important aspect that is often avoided is the supervisee/therapist's countertransference. It is crucial in supervision to develop comfort with countertransference.

Countertransference, which I define as the therapist's valence for being affected by their own and their patient's unconscious motives, is the tool best suited for re-finding lost objects that are central to understanding a patient's internal world. Ordinary emotional disturbances to the therapist's capacity for containment vary with each case. When containment is blocked, the therapist needs to reclaim her use of mentalization and emotional responsiveness to re-connect to the patient. The ability to use countertransference assumes that the therapist is well enough analyzed to retrieve parts of what has been confiscated. I have foolishly made this assumption, only to discover that it is often not the case. When supervisees feel stuck they may behave in compliant or defiant ways when feeling embarrassed or stupid. Supervision can be part of the problem, because unlike the doing of therapy, which is very private and subject to repression, the supervisor asks for an *in vivo* discussion of the therapy process, thereby exposing the blind spots of the therapist. I recommend warning new supervisees that learning will be painful due to the exposure of pitfalls and pratfalls, and vulnerability is inevitable in pursuit of clinical competence.

Patients rent out the mind of the analytic psychotherapist and transmit unconscious contents into it that the therapist can pick up and use to understand the patient (Heimann, 1950). By monitoring our own reactions, thoughts and feelings, we can detect and understand communications from patients, which they cannot recognize, because the communications have been transmitted unconsciously. This essential capacity for experiencing and monitoring countertransference as a standard part of technique to illuminate clinical understanding may fall beyond the scope of the supervisee. This leads to a dilemma in supervision. It is a fool's paradise to believe that process recordings, or recorded transcripts will objectify unconscious process. Supervisors know that there is no substitute or relief from imagining, emoting, regressing, and going bonkers from time to time in clinical work. What are our teaching options if a therapist is not well analyzed enough to bring to life the unconscious process through countertransference analysis? When the supervisee/therapist is unable to access this matrix of object relations, supervisor and supervisee/therapist have to invent or dream up the patient in order to experience the inside of the patient's world (Ogden, 2005). Together supervisor and supervisee/therapist dream up or invent a fiction, an approximation of the patient as felt and thought of by the therapist.

Utilizing such a freely associated approach to clinical supervision requires openness to emotional experience and suspension of certainties in favor of not understanding. If we accept the near impossibility of recreating an actual analytic session, supervisors can work on encouraging and modeling a range and depth for unconscious receptivity. Psychoanalytic supervision therefore requires much freedom, which can only occur alongside self discipline. When therapists are overwhelmed by their patients' unconscious material, they may strive too hard for change by offering a quick behavioral fix, or interfering with the transference. Their zealousness is a counter-resistance to the patient's resistance. The supervisor's internal subjective fantasies and feelings about the therapist locate the difficulties between the therapist and the patient not yet available to the therapist (Searles, 1965).

Training for supervisors

The training of therapists in the art of supervision is woefully lacking and unorganized. In current practice, supervisors often take on green and/or experienced therapists seeking private supervision not related to meeting institutional requirements. Whether the supervisor is experienced or new, unconscious motives, peer affiliations, prior training, and limited or no significant personal therapy combine to press him to collude in believing that supervision can provide all that is needed to overcome a combination of deficits.

Training institutes rely on senior faculty in appointing supervisors. Selection is based on reputation, and clinical skills. Courses on supervision theory and practice are usually not required. On the contrary, access to a growing knowledge base would prepare and guide new or experienced supervisors in the task of handing down psychoanalytic knowledge to the next generation of therapists. Tenure as a supervisor is no guarantee of special knowledge or ability. A modest preparation for supervisory work makes sense and at the very least supervisors need a self monitoring and supportive group experience in order to develop necessary awareness and skill.

External support for the supervisee

I know of situations where a supervisee was undertaking three supervisions of cases in treatment, but had only one session per week of personal therapy. In the case of another supervisee, her personal therapy or analysis occurred ten years prior to entering supervision, so that when personal issues arose, or an impasse in analytic thinking occurred, there was no therapist for back-up assistance in sorting things out. In one instance when it was suggested that a return to therapy would be helpful, the supervisee declined, saying she was finished being in therapy. Freud has suggested that analysts periodically return to analysis even for a few weeks, a suggestion few in our field follow.

Few therapists, outside the realm of institute requirements, are undertaking the stress and expense of psychoanalysis, preferring once a week therapy. They may spend shorter periods in treatment than they recommend for their private patients. Core issues may remain in the shadows, and then they are activated by clinical immersion with cases. Concern for economics may pair with narcissistic aims and naïveté to result in poor preparation for private practice. The supervisor who inherits the fall-out faces a *multifaceted* challenge.

Blurring of role and task in supervision

The supervisor has an educational role and a task of fostering clinical learning. At times, the clarity of role and task may become blurred by conscious anxiety about presenting one's clinical work and unconscious wishes that the supervisor fulfill a parental or therapeutic function instead. In properly case-focused supervision, conscious anxiety arises from the insecurity that the supervisee feels as she exposes the weaknesses in her psychotherapy technique and faces the impact of working with primitive mental content. Working with her patient, the supervisee/therapist enters the psychic space, the clinical mind field to which patient and therapist contribute, and anxieties are stirred. As the therapist in supervision pursues the unconscious meanings of case process, a myriad of reactions occur, and sometimes take on a life of their own. The border between self and other may become blurred, the supervisee/therapist needs help in recognizing what is occurring on the border, and supervision is needed to illuminate the issues and struggles. Reflection by supervisee and supervisor is needed for conducting and deepening the therapy, *and* for learning from supervision. The strain of these dual *reflecting processes* creates anxiety that the supervisee may or may not be well-enough analyzed to handle.

Sometimes under the strain, the therapist regresses, and then the supervisory relationship loses its case focus. The offer of supervision merges with unstated therapy needs, and the mental space of supervision becomes loaded with projective identifications. I am not suggesting that these circumstances automatically mean the supervisor or supervisee is suffering from unmetabolized deep pathology; although there are circumstances in which this does occur. I am implying that anxieties are certain to increase. Anxieties and defenses crop up in managing both relationships (supervisee and patient, supervisee and supervisor) and draw the two parties into the soup.

From the first meeting on, supervision can be affected by characterologically driven unconscious motives that drastically over determine how supervision will actually be used. I have encountered individual supervisees who challenge supervision as a teaching method by setting up the relationship to avoid being supervised at all, or who substitute experiences that render the supervision process null and void. In some instances the supervisee redirects their behavior towards enactments or acting out in the service of avoiding clinical learning. In less tumultuous situations there is a suspension of intellectual curiosity in learning from experience about clinical process in favor of a personal discussion of one's life problems. This may be turned to good use. Sometimes the sharing of a personal life situation in a trusted relationship with the supervisor may be a temporary diversion, and reflect a pre-conscious movement away from a difficult clinical situation; but in due course the material makes sense in amplifying countertransference in the case. Dream material may emerge that enriches understanding of the personal and clinical significance of the therapist's unconscious resonance. The avoidance I am referring to is more ego-syntonic and covert, continuing over time, and it is unrelated to case material. Discussion does not parallel, or eventually refer back to, the clinical case at hand so as to illuminate a blind spot of the therapist and remove an impasse. In the situations in which supervision is subverted, the supervisee's personal life experiences become the primary need, reflecting a use of supervision that changes the contractual arrangement to respond to an unacknowledged need for therapy. The supervisor has become the main transference outlet for a struggling therapist. There are circumstances in which no way can be found to analyze and re-direct this type of acting out, and, reluctantly, supervision has to be ended. Supervision is not to be therapy disguised as something else.

Case study

I will now offer a detailed report that illustrates an encounter with varying degrees of distortion and disturbance that threatened the process of learning. As in work with patients, the confidences of supervisees are of utmost concern. Case reporting, whether supervisory or clinical, requires that we carefully consider how to authentically present material to accomplish the learning task, without jeopardizing the anonymity of the therapist in supervision. So this report is carefully prepared to disguise the identity of the supervisee. In the situation under study the undermining of supervision was significant, and confrontation and clarification did not work. Re-connecting to the supervisory work required a creative move. The situation eventually improved, but I remain curious as to how others might have dealt with this supervisee/therapist.

Initial supervision meeting

Emily, (56) a clinical psychologist, had been in practice for ten years. She had no post-graduate psychoanalytic training, and supervision was limited to administrative handling of cases at the mental health center where she was employed. Emily proudly stated that she hosted educational meetings and book discussions for the clinical society at her home. I learned that she selected me based on having heard me speak at several conferences. She was impressed with my clinical discussions and object relations approach to difficult cases. She also commented I seemed warm and had a sense of humor. She worked 30 hours per week in a mental health agency, and now she was eager to develop her private practice, as many of her colleagues had done. She was locating her private practice in an office at the hospital assigned to her surgeon husband so that she had no rent or overhead, but also no waiting room.

Emily's first career had been in speech pathology, but after several years evaluating and working with children she decided to seek training in clinical psychology. Emily had two new referrals she wanted help with—a 12-year-old girl at her agency and a single adult schizoid man in her new practice. In discussing the frame of our supervisory contact, she told me that she wanted to attend supervision every other week. Since I always hold to weekly supervision, I asked her what her expectations about learning were, given the request for every other week. She said it was financial as she was just beginning in private practice. I admit that I could not help thinking about her new Mercedes parked in my back lot, and that her spouse was a surgeon.

I explained that with new supervisions weekly work was customary, and I was uncomfortable with any other arrangement, as I needed to learn about her work, and weekly case process would be a focus. With too much time between meetings the patient sessions would begin to add up, and little time would be available to freely discuss sessions in detail. Emily went along with my recommendation. I told her how I valued process writing, and she agreed to bring process notes.

Early course of supervision

Over the next three months Emily approached each session with a mixed agenda. Her case process note was written in long hand but lacked detail, and she never fully read what she had written. Although I was fine with anecdotal reports the lack of details left her material vague. She tended toward roping me into emotional discussions about private practice. She asked what do about having no waiting room, whether she had to soundproof her office like mine, what to do about fees, missed appointments, and insurance requirements, and how to get referrals. She also reported on her job at the clinic, complained that administrators and psychiatrists did not give her the respect she deserved in her position as a senior child therapist, and felt that no one listened to her recommendations about cases.

Other personal matters emerged. Feeling our supervision was giving her more confidence, she wanted to present cases at clinical society education meetings in hopes that this would lead to referrals, as it did for me. She referred to me as an inspiring role model. Emily was idealizing me, a tendency I viewed as a manipulation to make me feel special so that I would remain attentive to her every need. She wanted help to publish a case we were working on where Emily's patient was showing progress. The clinical society newsletter was soliciting articles on clinical topics. She believed she could do a good job having read many of her colleague's articles but appeared naïve about how to write an article. She did not ordinarily read clinical journals or books, but wanted to borrow some of mine, and asked me to copy some for her. I gave her a bibliography and one paper on the therapist's objects. She offered to pay me for editing time to assist her in writing her article, and we set that up. After two meetings Emily elected to put off completing the task in favor of presenting her case to a child therapy peer study group.

I was becoming uncomfortable in my role. Each situation not directly related to clinical learning was very important to her. Many of her topic questions were relevant to her professional aims, and I did feel that as her supervisor I should advise her on suitable arrangements for her practice as a context for learning to do good psychotherapy. So I would give a few minutes to address her requests before focusing on the case, and she was at first appreciative. She came to a decision that sharing with her husband was not professional enough, but each office that she looked at was too expensive or not good enough. My office, she decided was ideal, but she knew it was probably too expensive for her. I noticed that as time went on Emily took no action on any of my suggestions, perhaps because they involved taking initiative or investing money.

Six months went by. I had been tougher with Emily on the lack of clinical focus. I pointed out that many other issues seemed to be on her mind. I said that her preoccupation with them was pre-empting her skill development with her cases. I recommended using peers, real estate brokers, and private practice experts to help her arrange the context for her private practice but she did not follow up. Ambivalence was growing, mine and hers. The more she spoke of her concerns, the less committed to learning she was. She did not take in what I said, or how I said it, to increase her capacity for containment. In one session she went on about how her five-year-old grandson might be developmentally delayed and what did I think she could do about him. She wanted to be careful about respecting the boundaries with her rather clingy daughter and her son-in-law who thought of her as a know-it-all and with whom she had a strained relationship. I was not feeling successful during this time in supervision. I asked myself: What belongs in the supervision and what does not? As though she could read my mind, Emily blurted out that she might not have had enough personal therapy, her therapist having dropped her after twenty years with a short explanation. He had given all he could, and believed she knew enough to make it on her own.

What weighed heavily on my mind was that Emily wanted a lot, but narcissistic motives prevented Emily from following through. She rationalized in the face of insecurities or failures. She wanted rewards for talents not achieved by effort and found comfort and consolation in not following through. She used alibis to justify not being in role as a clinical supervisee and so she ignored both my input and her own conscious aims.

I was losing my interest in working with Emily and privately thought I had inherited her interrupted, indefinite 20-year therapy experience. Covert narcissistic collusion was very much alive and breeding in the supervision. I spoke of my concerns about her complex and varied use of me to contain a flooded feeling. I suggested that she might use additional therapy to re-work her previous abrupt termination. She declined, saying it would be too expensive. I persisted, explaining that she brought this up with me, and it must have some importance to have done so. What was it about? She said that it was too personal, and she shifted back to her case.

Amazing as it may seem, Emily's motives to accomplish better clinical work with child and adult cases was gradually bearing fruit, in spite of my growing intolerance for her covert moves. I supposed that her grandiose self mirrored a twin-ship with me as the competent other and that as long as she could sustain self-assurance in that way, our clinical discussions had a good effect.

Occasionally Emily referred to a discussion we had had. I was worried I might not otherwise reach her, and considered what else I was not considering that might bring us on line.

I was worn out by the cat and mouse game we were colluding in. I reminded her of her concerns about her grandson, and her daughter and son in law's reluctance to follow through on her ideas, and asked if she could see similar patterns in our conversations about her professional motives? She paid devoted lip service to my concerns, appearing meek and deferential. She could not examine her behavior and make the connections. I presented another overlap. Referring to her case material, I said that her schizoid patient appeared to hear everything she said about how he was avoiding engaging in life, and he did nothing about it. In her frustration she attempted to micro-manage him to no avail. She reported feeling useless, and limited in reaching him. I asked her about countertransference and re-capped her family situation. Emily listened and acknowledged she was angry at her patient, but she could not reflect on the larger countertransference implications. I told her that I was in a growing predicament about how to reach her so that she could see and learn from the not-so-coincidental dynamic resonance in the supervision. She was unable to respond to my self disclosure.

I pondered what to do. I recalled another therapist for whom reflecting on past personal therapy, her two marriages, and health issues helped illuminate countertransference issues in an integrative process that improved her clinical sensibilities. I was entirely comfortable with that therapist's way of learning, and it matched my frame in many other supervisions. I recognized that I was the type of supervisor that allowed personal material into supervision due to a preference for openness and an appreciation for serendipity and parallel process between therapist's valences and enactments. My frame had not consisted of a structured early checklist of one's personal treatment history, unconscious motives for supervision, and so forth; nor did I customarily explore the therapist's selection of me beyond standard motives. I permitted and encouraged exploring the layering of transferences. I also felt gratitude to all the mentors in my long career that supported my aims and efforts, and many had appreciated the parallel processes of personal and clinical transference. Their investments in me and dedication to my work were parts of my identity. These were important internalized objects for me to draw on.

A particular piece of theory also guided my supervisory approach— Klein's (1929) concept of projective identification in which a dissociative process can accompany extremes of idealization *and* bad object experiences. In supervision with Emily we had moved from idealization of me to denigration of most of what I offered her. This indicates severe splitting of the object. From a Kleinian perspective, splitting usually means a powerful interference of super-ego domi-nated hatred of an object that has disappointed and frustrated the self and its narcissistic aims.

Alone one evening at home, I mused, agonized, had a scotch and soda, and it then occurred to me: I was paying entirely too much attention to Emily. I was feeding her narcissistic aims. I grinned, and decided to ignore all and any issues or requests for non-clinical assistance. I made an assumption that underlying Emily's sense of entitlement there was a masochistic and guilty part of her. My plan was to stop feeding her unreasonable expectations in hope that unconscious guilt might re-direct her efforts to clinical learning. I did not expect conscious recognition or empathy to pour out. Integra-tion was not my goal. Education in supervision was my goal. If this approach did not work, I would discuss my limitations, and end our relationship with a clear conscience and a strong recommendation for therapy.

As I approached our next supervision I was very clear I had been holding Emily's ambivalences and procrastination about what she was willing to do in pursuit of private practice, publishing, and professional education. I had been feeding her considerable aims without success-fully challenging her ambivalences.

During the next session I held to my silence. Whenever she posed a non-clinical issue, I said nothing and waited. She tried valiantly sev-eral times to get me to collude, and I held back, attentive and wait-ing. She appeared exasperated but said nothing. After a few minutes a self-conscious look of embarrassment moved across her face. She paused, and, showing no indication of conscious insight, opposition, or displeasure, began to discuss her case. I was amazed at the shift. I was very uncomfortable not verbalizing the issues that imperiled her supervision. But I held to my plan. Silence had de-constructed our unconscious collusion.

Several months passed, and attentive silences had their effect. I even-tually asked Emily how she thought our work together was going. She stated she was more organized in preparing and discussing the case material and felt I was not interrupting her flow as much. I quietly took in the projection, nodded, and we went on with the work. Two years later Emily demonstrated case focused professionalism. Personal mat-ters hardly ever came into the setting. She voiced appreciation for the collaboration and appeared more comfortable with countertransference analysis to inform her clinical work.

Closing comments

Supervision remains an indispensable building block for psychoanalytic psychotherapy training. Properly conducted it enriches the self of the therapist in the pursuit of empathic-analytic capabilities. The supervision process always reveals psychic structure given its focus on unconscious material. To work at the optimum level, a supervisor takes on the role of the environmental mother, setting a frame that is respectful of development, aiming for reverie, and capable of working with the impact of multiple transference relationships. Object relations theory implies that if we wish to understand symptoms we should look for the company they keep. When building a play space is blocked, formidable difficulties arise as this case study shows, but they are not unusual as any study of supervision situations reveal. Unmetabolized unconscious forces in the supervision relationship challenged me to find a way to reach my supervisee, meet my educational goals, and preserve my integrity and sanity. In the triadic mental space of supervision, clinical work and supervision are significantly affected by unconscious processes of supervisor, supervisee, and supervisee's patient. Clear focus on task and boundary in supervision is essential for improving the learning and teaching of psychotherapy.

References

Bagnini, C. (2005). Supervision or space invader: Two's company and three makes for paranoid tendencies. In: Stadter, M. and Scharff, D. E., Eds. *Dimensions of Psychotherapy, Dimensions of Experience*, pp. 153–164. London: Routledge.

Heimann, P. (1950). On countertransference. *International Journal of Psycho-Analysis, 31*: 81–84.

Klein, M. (1929). Personification in the play of children. *International Journal of Psycho-Analysis, 10*: 193–204.

Ogden, T. (2005). On psychoanalytic supervision. *International Journal of Psycho-Analysis, 86*: 1265–80.

Searles, H. (1955). *The informational value of the supervisor's emotional experiences*. In: *Collected Papers on Schizophrenia and Related Subjects*, pp. 157–76. New York: International Universities Press, 1965.

CHAPTER FIVE

The supervision process in training

Rosa Maria Govoni and Patrizia Pallaro

W
e will present our theory and technique of supervision for therapists training in Dance Movement Therapy, practised at Art Therapy Italiana (ATI), a non-profit institute that provides training in art and dance therapy in Bologna. Our approach integrates classic dance/movement therapy training with the study of object relations theory of the British Independent School (Kohon, 1992). The creative modalities used in our supervisory setting are: movement, gesture, and dance. The complex task of supervision within the ATI Dance Movement Therapy psychodynamic training program involves linking specific theories to the clinical material presented, and then supporting specific methods of intervention to help therapists aid patients in the exploration of their experiences. As we develop the therapist's understanding of clinical issues and related therapeutic interventions, we bring to awareness transference and countertransference themes and elucidate unconscious motivations and healing phantasies present in both patient and therapist. We open up the therapists to finding ways to creatively spark their patients' growth. All this needs to occur in an emotionally safe space in which both therapists and patients are respected for their hard work.

Movement, words, imagination, creativity, self-reflection and analysis, all contribute to the rich psychological interplay between therapist and supervisor and the parallel process referred from the therapist's relationship with her patient. Body expression facilitates access to that *potential space* in which transformative events can take place at the threshold between internal and external reality, as indicated by Winnicott (1965, 1971). The capacity to symbolize is fostered by allowing unconscious communication between patient and therapist (or therapist and supervisor) to surface. We effect this by engaging the therapist's creative process in response to unconscious communication, developing movement and body based interventions, then verbalizing the co-constructed experience. The goal is the integration of body and psyche in both patient and therapist.

Movement therapy techniques and curriculum

To foster the dance movement therapist's understanding of psychological process as it relates to and informs bodily expression and meaning in training, clinical practice and supervision, we use the following specific instruments from the field of movement. We will list them below specifically for the reader who is a movement therapist. Psychotherapists reading this chapter who are not familiar with these techniques, will recognize some elements of the curriculum and will be able to follow our integration of psychotherapy and movement techniques when we give vignettes from supervisees later in the chapter.

• Laban Movement Analysis, integrated by Bartenieff Fundamentals (Laban, 1950; Bartenieff & Lewis, 1980);
• Kestenberg Studies and Movement Profile (Kestenberg, 1973; Kestenberg & Sossin, 1979; Lewis & Loman, 1990; Kestenberg Amighi et al., 1999);
• Authentic Movement process (Adler, 1985, 2002; Chodorow, 1991, 1998; Wyman-McGinty, 1998, 2005; Pallaro, 2000, in press).

To be more specific, we use a technique called *moving through polarities*, as Laban indicated in his effort-shape theory, using the Laban's *cube* or *drives*, (Bartenieff & Lewis, 1980, p. 91) and specific exercises, called *fundamentals* (Bartenieff & Lewis, 1980, p. 229). We use *improvisation of movement* in relationship to an image or feeling in order to work through countertransferential material. Supervisors use these techniques from movement therapy to open trainees' awareness and consciousness in preparation for in-depth therapeutic work with their patients.

In the supervisory process we expand on the topics taught in our integrated curriculum, as follows:

- The study of the creative process, aesthetic experience and development of symbol formation, understanding of unconscious phantasies and their functions as well as analysis of the various developmental phases, each with their characteristics and specific roles (Klein, 1932, 1958, 1961; Segal, 1957; Milner, 1969; Kestenberg, 1973; Bollas, 1989; Chodorow, 1991; Alvarez, 1992);
- An understanding of the matrix of the body and its kinaesthetic nature, its unconscious reverberations, and unmentalized experience (Schilder, 1950; Whitehouse, 1963; Chaiklin, 1975; Dosamantes Alperson, 1980; Bernstein, 1984, 1986; Adler, 1985; Chodorow, 1991; Wyman-McGinty, 1998, 2005);
- An awareness of the functions that the *intermediate area, transitional object and psyche/soma* play in the relationship between patient and therapist or between therapist and supervisor (Winnicott, 1965, 1971; Milner, 1969; Bram & Gabbard, 2001; Thomas, 2005);
- The observation of both characteristic normal and pathological developmental stages and phases (Klein, 1932; Erikson, 1950; Bick, 1964; Freud, 1965; Stern, 1985; Gaddini, 1987; Sowa, 1999);
- A deepening understanding of transference and countertransference phenomena, particularly in their somatic manifestations, and how the embodied experience manifests in the patient (or patients), therapist, and supervisor (Heimann, 1950; Racker, 1968; Ogden, 1982, 1997, 2005; Momigliano & Robutti, 1992; Scharff, D., 1992; Scharff & Scharff, 1998; Wyman-McGinty, 1998, 2005; Becker & Seibel, 2005; Pallaro, in press).

Culture and ethnic background always frame these processes and imbue our experiences with different meanings (Foulks & Schwartz, 1982; Pallaro, 1993, 1997; Bonovitz, 2005). Therefore, awareness of culturally based stereotyping, ethnocentrisms and expectations, understanding of ethnically determined verbal as well as non-verbal communications, whether consciously or unconsciously expressed, are of vital importance in the therapeutic endeavour (Pallaro, 1997).

This integrated curriculum was developed specifically to aid our students in comprehending movement expression as a form of primary organization and codification of psychic experience in the pre-verbal phases of human development (Klein, 1932, 1958, 1961; Stern, 1985; Schore, 1999; Wyman-McGinty, 2005). Special attention is devoted to the understanding of how movement and embodied experience foster neurological as well as psychological growth (Winnicott, 1965; Stern, 1985; Berrrol, 1992; Schore, 1999; Wyman-McGinty, 1998, 2005; Fonagy, Gergely, Jurist & Target, 2002).

Learning to create a safe space for therapy

Our students are trained to provide their patients with a safe and secure environment. They learn to pay close attention to their patients' needs, desires, longings, personal characteristics, and potential growth capabilities, all in the service of fostering a secure sense of self. Students practice making conscious use of movement as an analytic tool, in order to grasp the complexity of what is exchanged between patient and therapist. In their own therapy, experiential training, and supervised practicum, they learn to read the meaning embedded in a movement, a body posture, a sensation, an affectively charged word. Students make conscious use of the body as a receptive instrument for kinaesthetic empathy, proprioceptive knowledge and imagination, the discernment and containment of crucial aspects of their somatic countertransferential experiences (Pallaro, 2007).

Trainees are also expected to develop the ability to respect *self* and *other*, each with their unique presence and original characteristics. We expect them to open themselves to the unknown and withstand the ensuing tension. We help them to enter the realm of potential space and transitional phenomena with neither judgement nor expectations, so that the creative process can unfold and manifest its complex interweaving patterns of relationship (Bion, 1970; Adler, 1985; Bram & Gabbard, 2001; Driver, 2002a; Thomas, 2005). Further, students are encouraged to delve into their personal psychological development so as to augment their capability to sustain and relate to their dissociated, disavowed, repressed, inhibited or split off parts (Dosamantes, 1992; Chodorow, 1991).

The supervision setting as a learning alliance

The supervision setting facilitates and supports a learning alliance—not a therapeutic relationship but one in which an open and receptive attitude toward deeper emotional intelligence is encouraged. The supervisory frame enables the development of the capacity to access preconscious and unconscious levels of experience and, most importantly, to take into account each supervisee's individuality, spontaneity and creativity (Meltzer, 1979; Resnik, 1995; Ferro, 1999; Driver, 2002a; Bolognini, 2003; Chasserguet-Smirgel, 2005; Martin, 2005; Ogden, 2005; Thomas, 2005).

The concept of the supervisory *frame* or *holding* implies clear and definite boundaries about what a learning experience is, as opposed to what a therapeutic intervention might be (Sarnat, 1992; Driver, 2002a). The supervisor is a teacher, not a therapist. The supervisor's task is to hold everything that may surface during supervision without succumbing to the temptation of trying to treat it (Godbout, 2004). Using tact and clinical sensitivity, the supervisor may refer the supervisee for personal therapy in order to promote further personal development (Sarnat, 1992; Stewart, 2002; Becker & Seibel, 2005). Within the supervisory frame, the supervisees can reveal their learning styles, needs, capacities and deficits in relating to their patients. The supervisor will notice these in the first paragraphs of a case presentation and the selective presentation of demographic data. As the supervision proceeds, the supervisor will see the problem areas again in the discussion of issues regarding the therapeutic frame and in the analysis of the emotional and symbolic content of the patient's verbal material and movement expressions.

Presentation of a clinical case in supervision may uncover problematic areas in the trainee's development as a therapist and alert the supervisor to raise specific questions aimed at deepening the relationship between patient and therapist. Using an analytical approach, supervisors help supervisees by posing questions that relate to technique, interpretation, transference and countertransference, as they pertain to their patients' movement patterns. It is crucial to a well-rounded development of the therapist-in-training to notice and explore the multi-layered issues arising from reflection and analysis. For example, questions such as the following may arise:

- What healing fantasies may underlie a particular intervention on the part of the supervisee?
- How does the supervisee deal with her desire to cure another person?
- How does the supervisee attempt to deal with those of her own life experiences which might interfere with or hinder treatment?

- Does the supervisee's unconscious longing to be healed motivate her interventions?
- How does the supervisee's present or past personal analysis or psychotherapy enter into the therapeutic, supervisory and learning process?
- What are the supervisee's fantasies about what helps and what hinders treatment?
- How does the supervisee deal with her patient's transference towards her and, in turn, how does she deal with her own transference towards her supervisor and the institution within which they operate?

The therapist-in-training does not operate in a vacuum. The supervisee-supervisor dyad is a mutually affecting relationship, so the same questions apply to the supervisor (Ungar & Bush De Ahumada, 2001). We encourage supervisors to pose and reflect on these issues in group and individual consultations (Driver, 2002b). All levels of dyadic engagement (therapist/patient, supervisee/supervisor, supervisor/institution, supervisor/training program, supervisee/institution, supervisee/training program, supervisor/patient and all other possible combinations) are taken into account and, hopefully, processed (Yerushalmi, 1999).

Within the supervisory relationship, the learning alliance usually follows a developmental process (Driver, 2002a). The supervisor attunes to the supervisee's level of clinical experience, embraces the theories and modalities most familiar to the supervisee, and accepts the therapeutic contract established in the clinical setting/organization in which the supervisee works. Synergy is established between supervisor and supervisee by sharing movements and their meaning connected to words and thoughts, thus creating the deep understanding and self-knowledge that only body language can contain and make manifest. The non-judgmental atmosphere created by the supervisor assures supervisees that whatever is revealed by their bodily expressions is part of the clinical work and will not be analysed in terms of the supervisee's life experiences or particular problems. Students are required to commit, throughout the course of the training, to acknowledge that whatever may surface in supervision must then be faced in their personal therapy (and not avoided) in order to understand its clinical relevance for their patients' treatment.

No matter what modality is chosen to introduce a particular case, special attention is given to the nonverbal mode of communication with which supervisees share information regarding their engagement in the therapeutic relationship (Jacobs, 1994). Supervisors must be able to attune to their students' communication styles and engage in their own self-reflections and analyses in order to understand the parallel processes operative within the patient–therapist dyad, the supervisor–supervisee dyad, the supervisor-training program dyad, the therapist-agency dyad etc.

Dance Movement Therapy, play, and the creative arts therapies approach

Students' past experiences in dance and movement, and specifically Dance Movement Therapy training, exposure to working with different clinical populations, personal therapy, practice with other art forms, and creative endeavours in general, shape the background knowledge from which a clinical case is presented. The creative arts approach focuses on the supervisees' process of reporting their patients' movement phrases, significant postures, gestures, all expressed in role-playing enactments which pinpoint conscious and unconscious material made manifest through sensations, feelings and thoughts. Supervisees' becoming aware of their own experience, as it is made manifest through their bodies, supports the process of tracing emotional and symbolic content and relating it to patients' themes and dynamics.

Using dance, movement and gesture enables the supervisor to understand resistances, defences, projections and projective identifications expressed in nonverbal communication (Jacobs, 1994; Becker & Seibel, 2005). Transference and countertransference, with special attention to somatic countertransference (Pallaro, 2007) are also addressed through dance, movement and gesture. All are elements of the therapeutic relationship to be examined for the benefit of the patient. The field of play and movement supports creative, long lasting learning (Winnicott, 1971). Hawkins and Shohet (1989) comment: "In the supervision that we give we try and create a climate which avoids the sense of expert and student both studying the client 'out there' and instead create a 'play space' in which the dynamics and pressures of the work can be felt, explored and understood; and where new ways of working can be co-created by both supervisor and supervisees working together" (p. 7).

The supervision process

The supervisor's creativity finds its way in the interplay of primary and secondary processes, through extremely detailed attention on movements, feelings, sensations and images. Supervisors listen to the clinical history and explore the clinical rationale for treatment. They set the treatment in the context of the therapist's contract with the provider institution in which the supervised therapy is provided and with the training program in which the supervisee is enrolled. They notice how these flow and shift in the larger context of various therapeutic processes, interventions, and institutional contracts. They shift their overall attention from outer realities impinging upon treatment to inner processes and phenomena, including their own somatic countertransferential cues.

Supervisors carefully monitor their tendencies to over-stimulate and over-feed their supervisees. They focus on establishing a learning alliance by helping their supervisees to recognize psychological dynamics and movement themes, which may promote or obstruct their work with patients. Movement analysis is used to observe what the supervisee brings at a movement level, in the body. Verbal descriptions of sessions and session themes as well as dialogues between patient(s) and therapist are also scrutinized. If supervisees are not well aware of their own defences and personal issues, problematic dynamics may emerge from patients' conscious or unconscious material and communications. Movement is used in various ways to reveal these unconscious messages, often embedded in projective identifications, which are frequently disturbing to the supervisee. Whether it is a body image disturbance, a physical pain, difficulty in the expression of a developmental movement pattern or tension flow rhythm, the supervisor will initiate the movement work in the supervisory setting in order to help supervisees in the deconstruction of hidden communications, gentle dismantling of bodily defences, and recognition of psychological obstacles or collusive relationships.

Training in Authentic Movement for the Dance Movement Therapist supervisor supports development of further clinical sensitivity. It hones supervisors' skills to hold conflictual material, to discern transference and countertransferential cues as well as increase their capacity to make choices which will benefit their supervisees' development and growth (Driver, 2002a; Becker & Seibel, 2005; Pallaro, 2007) as well as, of course, their supervisees' patients.

Instruments, techniques, methods, and goals of supervision

The use of Laban's (1950) and Bartenieff's (1980) techniques, which prepare for the engagement of perceptive attention and observation (Gendlin, 1978; Dosamantes Alperson, 1980; Deikman, 1982; Aposhyan, 2004), ground supervisees in a deep experience of their bodies, allowing kinesthetic sensations and feelings to arise in an environment of safety. Therapists-in-training become subtly aware of those deep connections, which enables them to offer intervention strategies which may elicit profound psychological transformations in their patients, especially those who present as extremely regressed, severely ill or low functioning (Wyman-McGinty, 1998). Sometimes it is useful to experiment with role-playing (La Barre, 2001), which allows students to access their patients' inner dynamics and transference and their own countertransferential material en route to understanding their own unconscious healing phantasies.

All supervisors in the program have been trained in, and practice, Authentic Movement regularly. Authentic Movement training is introduced in the third year of the four-year curriculum. Elements of Authentic Movement are used to increase knowledge and awareness of projective mechanisms. The practice of Authentic Movement (Adler, 1985, 2002; Chodorow, 1998; Wyman-McGinty, 1998, 2005; Pallaro, 2007) further enables students to open up to and yet be able to remain in that difficult emotional place of *not knowing* (Bion, 1970; Adler, 1985; Pallaro, 2007; Yorke, 2005). Students develop the capacity to trust that an image aiding the therapeutic process may arise, that a sensation connecting their experiences to those of their patients may appear, and that a thought or insight rooted in their kinesthetic experiences may elicit valid interpretations (McCall, 1986; Musicant, 1994, 2001; Pallaro, 2007).

In individual supervision role-playing is usually done by the supervisee but the supervisor may also take an active part in it. In group supervision, each member presents a case in a pre-determined rotation. Authentic Movement is used along with role-playing structures, which vary with the group's need. In group supervision there is more space (physical, mental and emotional) to use different forms of creative exploration while role-playing. In the group setting, therapists-in-training may become conscious of their own personal desire to heal and to be healed. Each member presents the issues in a clinical case, and is then encouraged to play the parts of both patient

and therapist, at different times. Themes related to the healing patient/
therapist couple will emerge, allowing the supervisor and the group to
work as a *resonance body* (Nikolitsa, 2002) in a supporting yet differenti-
ated manner, concentrating at times on specific issues in order to help
supervisees become aware of their countertransference and discern
projections and projective or introjective identifications. To be open and
receptive to the group mind and resonance body allows therapists-in-
training to discover new ways to promote reparative experiences and
to offer appropriate creative interventions in the therapeutic work with
their patients.

Dance Movement Therapy training group and choreography

A Dance Movement Therapy group supervision session may be likened
to a choreographed dance. Supervision comprises components of the
dance: the invisible dancer (patient) made visible in the body of the
therapist (supervisee), the chorus (her fellow colleagues), and the audi-
ence (supervisor). When positions and movements change in the dance,
hunches and insights may occur. Supervisees may be able to shed light
on their unconscious processes, thus gathering further thoughts or dis-
covering other movements which may prove fruitful in the therapeutic
endeavour with their patients.

The supervisee presenting the case in group supervision is flanked
by colleagues who, taking turns, choreograph different movement or
body interventions in response to their bodily felt experiences as they
emerge from their own reactions to the material presented. Or, embody-
ing the patient's themes, stance, and movements, the chorus is made to
move by the supervisee's directions and suggestions while the supervisee is engaged (through the so-called split attention process) in her own
bodily felt experience first, followed by that of her patient (Dosamantes
Alperson, 1980; Caldwell, 1997; Pallaro, 2007). The supervisor moves in
and out, on and off the stage, sometimes offering her own bodily felt
experience as counterpoint, other times offering verbal suggestions, if
deemed appropriate. At other moments, questions are formulated in
order to discover the differences between two movement sequences
and their induced reactions or to probe further about the supervisee's
personal ideas, images, judgements, projections, blocks or emerging
bodily felt sensations.

In the final section of the dance, all supervisees pause in order to process the material that has emerged and allow for the re-integration of new insights. All engage in inquiring into, for example, what the body feels it needs to do after this process and what the dance tells us about the patient, the therapist, and ourselves. A composite picture of the patient/therapist-in-training dyad is thus created. Hopefully new ideas will surface from this dance which will in turn aid the supervisee in focusing on the next intervention needed to get the therapeutic relationship to move forward.

Vignette from a supervisee

"After one of my sessions with a borderline patient I remember the strange body feeling of much pain in my left arm and upper trunk, as if I were having a stroke, and a subtle rage lasted all day. In the supervision group in which I presented this material, the supervisor asked me to instruct two colleagues to play a typical scene occurring in therapy with that patient. They enacted the scene while I observed. At one point, the supervisor asked me to sit down and feel my trunk, feeling the shape/posture I was in, and then to release some of the tension by exhaling [a technique called *shape flow support breath*]. This allowed me to really feel what I was seeing. I saw the destructive behaviour of my colleague in the role of the patient and the masochistic conduct of the one in the role of the therapist. I felt a lot of anger. At that moment, a personal memory surfaced while the sharp pain in my upper chest and left side disappeared. I realized then how much rage I was holding on behalf of my patient, seemingly spilling it into me, and how difficult it was for me to be aware of it so that it could be properly contained and metabolized."

"Further work in my own therapy allowed me to work through my rage, which was blocking my clinical understanding. Through supervision, I realized I had identified with her rage and was resonating with it, caught in a strong projective identification, holding feelings my patient could not feel at that moment. Later in treatment, my patient felt safe enough to disclose her constant fear that her mother would die of a stroke because of her incompetence. Further concomitant work in supervision allowed me to search and find better treatment interventions for my patient, who certainly needed more containment and a therapist who could openly withstand her attacks and fear."

The training group, a protected and open territory for expression, offers an opportunity for students to move in a self-directed manner and get in touch with conscious and unconscious motivations for movement. Immediately after the group has moved for about 30 or 40 minutes in a self-directed manner, with no suggestions whatsoever coming from the supervisor who is leading the group, the supervisor asks students to select a movement phrase they have found to be particularly significant and to repeat it a number of times. Dyads are formed: one person takes the witness position, the other the mover. The two alternately move their movement phrases in the presence of each other. The therapist-in-training, who was the mover in each sequence, speaks first while the other offers her witnessing. Every dyad does this at the same time in different places in the room.

In this supervision structure, one objective is to sharpen the awareness of judgmental opinions and biases as these emerge from both the witnessing and the moving experiences in another's presence, be it the supervisor/supervisee dyad or the therapist/patient dyad. This practice invariably touches upon various transference and countertransference issues. Supervisees are asked to honestly respond to questions such as:

- Did your movement change when being witnessed by the other?
- How did it change?
- Did you notice anything changing in your body as you witnessed?
- What did you perceive (if anything): a body sensation, an urge to move, a feeling?
- Did you see an image in your mind's eye?
- How does this experience relate to the case presented?

Such work on focusing and awareness helps trainees comprehend their projections and relationship patterns in response to specific events or encounters. They discover from inside themselves what kind of therapeutic strategies they feel comfortable implementing or challenged in executing.

Vignette from a supervisee

"In my internship in a private institution, I saw a very disturbed eight year old child twice a week. He was driving me crazy, running all over me and spitting on me any time I would try to stop him, screaming and banging things against the radiators in order to make louder noises, and throwing pencils and pens around, anything he could get his hands on.

"Although I had organized the room in a special way just for him, emptying it of all the things he could break, placing cushions that could be thrown around without damaging anything or anybody, one day, this boy goes behind a curtain and finds a drinking glass (which unfortunately I had not noticed before) and breaks it right away. The glass goes into a thousand pieces. Now we can really hurt ourselves. I scream "Stop!" and really stare at him, feeling not at all like a therapist, afraid that we will hurt each other. I yell at him to stay really still until I finish cleaning the floor. He does remain still. Clearing the floor takes me a long time. I feel despair. I do not want to work with him anymore. I am not capable of this. The floor is finally clear. Yet I keep telling him to be still. Finally it is time for him to go.

"In my supervision group, one day I presented this case and spoke of my countertransference and my feeling of utter despair in his presence. I was encouraged to move with my peers as witnesses and to wait for images to emerge which could help me in those moments of feeling so lost and not knowing what to do next.

"I find myself back in the psychotherapy room. I'm sitting on the floor, silent, not responding to any word or sound the boy utters. Then an image comes of a big, strong guard, a soldier at the edge of a fort. As this image emerges, the fact that this child is always doing things he is not supposed to comes to my mind. I can picture now the psychotherapy room as that fort, as a space in which I can stand guard for his safety, and for my own safety. He can use this fort as a solid base to approach his non-violent self and recover his ability to play again as a soldier or a fighting boy, beside me.

"I embody that image and start moving it. I become that very strong soldier, that big, strong, bonded, grounded guard, who steadily walks at the edge of the fort and by doing so defines a safe space with definite limits. I also begin to talk as that guard with a loud, strong and direct voice. I understand now what I need to do in order to help this boy be safe and develop impulse control."

Conclusion

Supervision in a psychodynamically oriented dance movement therapy training calls for a profound, trusting, creative relationship between trainees and supervisors. The supervisor functions as a container for different layers of experiences lived by the supervisees, all of which must be seen, recognized, analysed, and used to foster the therapists-in-training's learning and growth. Body and movement are instruments that are used to allow supervisees and supervisors into contact with manifest and latent dynamics intrinsic to the therapist/patient relationship. These elements need to be recognized as communications of the inner world of the patient. The supervisor helps the trainee process and metabolize these communications so that, when decoded and transformed, they can foster patients' awareness, growth and recovery. This direct physical, mental and emotional approach to supervision allows the trainees to integrate their theoretical, clinical and experiential knowledge. Movement, gesture and dance, imagination, and self-reflection on the direct experience of supervisee and supervisor are the essential components of this creative process of supervision.

References

Adler, J. (1985). Who is the witness? A description of Authentic Movement. In: P. Pallaro, Ed. (2000). *Authentic Movement: Essays by Mary Starks Whitehouse, Janet Adler and Joan Chodorow* (2nd. ed.). pp. 141–159. London: Jessica Kingsley Publishers.

Adler, J. (2002). *Offering from the conscious body: The discipline of Authentic Movement*. Rochester, VT: Inner Traditions.

Alvarez, A. (1992). *Live Company: Psychoanalytic Therapy With Autistic, Abused and Borderline Psychotic Children*. London: Routledge.

Aposhyan, S. (2004). *Body-Mind Psychotherapy: Principles, Techniques, and Practical Applications*. New York: W. W. Norton.

Bartenieff, I. & Lewis, D. (1980). *Body Movement: Coping with the environment*. New York: Gordon and Breach.

Becker, B. & Seibel, J. (2005). Becoming Better Supervisors. Proceedings from the 40th Annual ADTA Conference: American Rhythms/International Rhythms. Dance/Movement Therapy Practice and Research. Columbia, MD: ADTA.

Bernstein, P. L. (1984; 1986). *Theoretical Approaches in Dance Movement Therapy. Vols. I & II*. Dubuque, Iowa: Kendall/Hunt.

Berrol, C. (1992). The Neurophysiologic Basis of the Mind-Body Connection in Dance/Movement Therapy. *American Journal of Dance Therapy*, 14(1): 19–29.

Bick, E. (1964). Notes on infant observation in psycho-analytic training. *International Journal of Psycho-Analysis, 45*: 558–566.

Bion, W. R. (1970). *Attention and Interpretation.* London: Tavistock Publications.

Bollas, C. (1989). *The Shadow of the Object: Psychoanalysis of the Unthought Unknown.* New York: Columbia University Press.

Bolognini, S. (2003). *Psychoanalytic Empathy.* London: Free Associations Books.

Bonovitz, C. (2005). Locating culture in the psychic field: Transference and countertransference as cultural products. *Contemporary Psychoanalysis, 41*(1): 55–75.

Bram, A. D. & Gabbard, G. O. (2001). Potential space and reflective functioning. *International Journal of Psycho-Analysis, 821*: 685–699.

Caldwell, C. (1997). The moving cycle. In C. Caldwell, (Ed.). *Getting in Touch.* pp. 101–116. Wheaton, IL: Quest Books.

Chaiklin, H. (Ed.). (1975). *Marian Chace: Her papers.* Columbia, MD: ADTA.

Chasseguet-Smirgel, J. (2005). *The Body as Mirror of the World.* London: Free Associations Books.

Chodorow, J. (1991). *Dance Therapy and Depth Psychology: The Moving Imagination.* London: Routledge.

Deikman, A. J. (1982). *The Observing Self: Mysticism and Psychotherapy.* Boston: Beacon Press.

Dosamantes, I. (1992). The intersubjective relationship between therapist and patient: A key to understanding denied and denigrated aspects of the patient's self. *The Arts in Psychotherapy, 19*: 359–365.

Dosamantes, I. & Alperson, E. (1980). Contacting bodily-felt experiencing in psychotherapy. In: J. E. Shorr, G. E. Sobel, P. Robin, & J. A. Connella (Eds.) *Imagery: Its many dimensions and applications.* pp. 223–250. New York: Plenum.

Driver, C. (2002a). The geography and topography of supervision in a group setting. In: C. Driver & Martin, E. (Eds.). *Supervising Psychotherapy.* pp. 85–96. London: Sage Publications.

Driver, C. (2002b). Internal states in the supervisory relationship. In: C. Driver & Martin, E. (Eds.). *Supervising Psychotherapy.* pp. 51–63. London: Sage Publications.

Erikson, E. (1950/1963). *Childhood and Society.* New York: Norton.

Ferro, A. (1999). *The Bi-Personal Field.* London: Routledge.

Fonagy, P., Gergely, G. Jurist, E. & Target, M. (2002). *Affect Regulation, Mentalization, and the Development of Self.* New York: Other Press.

Foulks, E. F., & Schwartz, F. (1982). Self and object: Psychoanalytical perspectives in cross-cultural fieldwork and interpretation. *Ethos, 10*(3): 254–278.

Freud A. (1965). Normality and pathology in childhood: Assessments of development. In: *The Writings of Anna Freud, (vol. 6)*. New York: International University Press.

Gaddini, R. (1987). Early care and the roots of internalization. *International Review of Psycho-Analysis, 1*: 321–333.

Gendlin, E. T. (1978). *Focusing*. New York: Bantam Books.

Godbout, C. (2004). Reflections on Bion's 'elements of psychoanalysis' Experience, thought and growth. *International Journal of Psycho-Analysis, 85*: 1123–1236.

Goleman, D. (1996). *The Meditative Mind*. New York: Tarcher & Putnam.

Hawkins, P. & Shohet, R. (1989). *Supervision in The Helping Professions*. Philadelphia: Open University Press.

Heimann, P. (1950). On countertransference. *International Journal of Psycho-Analysis, 31*: 81–84.

Jacobs, T. J. (1994). Nonverbal communications: some reflections on their role in the psychoanalytic process and psychoanalytic education. *Journal of the American Psychoanalytic Association, 42*: 741–762.

Kestenberg, J. S. (1973). *Children and Parents: Psychoanalytic studies in development*. New York: Aronson.

Kestenberg, J. S. & Sossin, K. (1979). *The Role of Movement Pattern in Development*. Vol. I and II. New York: Dance Notation Bureau.

Kestenberg Amighi, J., Loman, S., Lewis, P., Sossin, M. K. (1999). *OPA— The Meaning of Movement: Developmental and Clinical Perspectives of the Kestenberg Movement Profile*. New York: Gordon and Breach.

Klein, M. (1932). *The Psycho-Analysis of Children*. London: Hogarth Press.

Klein, M. (1958). On the development of mental functioning. *International Journal of Psycho-Analysis, 39*: 84–90.

Klein, M. (1961). *Narrative of a Child Analysis*. London: Hogarth Press.

Kohon, G. (1992). *The British School of Psychoanalysis: The Independent Tradition*. London: Free Association Books.

La Barre, F. (2001). *On Moving and Being Moved*. Hillsdale, NJ: The Analytic Press.

Laban, R. (1950). *The Mastery of Movement*. London: MacDonald & Evans.

Lewis, P. & Loman, S. (1990). *The Kestenberg Movement Profile: Its past, present applications and future directions*. New Hampshire: Antioch England Graduate School.

Martin, E. (2005). The unconscious in supervision. In: C. Driver & Martin, E. (Eds.). *Supervision and the Analytic Attitude*. pp. 3–33. London: Whurr Publications.

McCall, D. (1986). Personal communication.

Meltzer, D. (1979). *Sexual States of Mind*. London: Karnac Books.

Milner, M. (1969). *The Hands of the Living God: An Account of a Psychoanalytic Treatment*. London: Hogarth.

Momigliano, N. L. & Robutti, A. (1992). *Shared Experience: The Psychoanalytic Dialogue.* London: Karnac Books.

Musicant, S. (1994). Authentic Movement in clinical work. In: P. Pallaro (Ed.) (2007) *Authentic Movement: Moving the Body, Moving the Self, Being Moved.* London: Jessica Kingsley.

Musicant, S. (2001). Authentic Movement: Clinical and theoretical considerations. In: P. Pallaro (Ed.) (2007) *Authentic Movement: Moving the Body, Moving the Self, Being Moved.* London: Jessica Kingsley.

Nikolitsa, A. (2002). *Capturing and utilising the somatic countertransferential phenomena: An heuristic attempt.* Unpublished master's thesis, Laban Centre, London, UK.

Ogden, T. (1982). *Projective Identification and Psychotherapeutic Technique.* Northvale, NJ: Jason Aronson.

Ogden, T. (1997). *Reverie and Interpretation: Sensing something Human.* Northvale, NJ: Jason Aronson.

Ogden, T. (2005). On psychoanalytic supervision. *International Journal of Psycho-Analysis, 86*: 1265–1280.

Pallaro, P. (1993). Culture, self, and body-self: Dance/Movement therapy across cultures. In: F. J. Bejjani (Ed.). *Current Research in Arts Medicine.* pp. 287–291. Chicago: a cappella books.

Pallaro, P. (1997). Culture, self and body-self: Dance/Movement Therapy with Asian Americans. *The Arts in Psychotherapy, 24*(3): 227–241.

Pallaro, P. (Ed.). (2000). *Authentic Movement: Essays by Mary Starks Whitehouse, Janet Adler and Joan Chodorow* (2nd. ed.). London: Jessica Kingsley Publishers.

Pallaro, P. (2007). Somatic countertransference: The therapist in relationship. In: P. Pallaro (Ed.) (2007). *Authentic Movement: Moving the Body, Moving the Self, Being Moved.* London: Jessica Kingsley.

Racker, H. (1968). *Transference and countertransference.* New York: International Universities Press.

Resnik, S. (1995). *Mental Space.* London: Karnac Books.

Sarnat, J. E. (1992). Supervision in relationship: Resolving the teach-treat controversy in psychoanalytic supervision. *Psychoanalytic Psychology, 9*: 387–403.

Scharff, J. S. (1992). *Projective and Introjective Identification and the Use of the Therapist's Self.* Northvale, NJ: Jason Aronson.

Scharff, J. S. & Scharff, D. E. (1998). The geography of transference and countertransference. In: *Object Relations Individual Therapy.* pp. 241–281. Northvale, NJ: Jason Aronson.

Schilder, P. F. (1950). *The Image and Appearance of the Human Body.* London: Kegan Paul, Trench & Trubner.

Schore, A. (1999). *Affect Regulation and the Origin of the Self: The Neurobiology of Emotional Development.* New York: Lawrence Erlbaum Associates.

Segal, H. (1957). Notes on symbol formation. *International Journal of Psycho-Analysis, 38*: 391–397.

Sowa, A. (1999). Observing the unobservable: The Tavistock Infant Observation Model and its relevance to clinical training. *Fort da, 5*(1). Retrieved from http://www.fortda.org/Spring_99/Observing.html.

Stern, D. N. (1985). *The Interpersonal World of the Human Infant.* New York: Basic Books.

Stewart, J. (2002). The interface between teaching and supervision. In: C. Driver & Martin, E. (Eds.). *Supervising Psychotherapy.* pp. 64–83. London: Sage Publications.

Thomas, M. (2005). Through the looking glass: Creativity in supervision. In C. Driver & Martin, E. (Eds.). *Supervision and the Analytic Attitude.* pp. 115–129. London: Whurr Publications.

Ungar, V. R. & Bush De Ahumada, L. (2001). Supervision: A container-contained approach. *International Journal of Psycho-Analysis, 82*: 71–81.

Whitehouse, M. S. (1963). Physical movement and personality. In: P. Pallaro, (Ed). (2000). *Authentic Movement: Essays by Mary Starks Whitehouse, Janet Adler and Joan Chodorow* (2nd. ed.). pp. 51–57. London: Jessica Kingsley Publishers.

Winnicott, D. W. (1965). *The Maturational Processes and the Facilitating Environment.* New York: International University Press.

Winnicott, D. W. (1971). *Playing and Reality.* New York: Basic Books.

Wyman-McGinty, W. (1998). The body in analysis: Authentic Movement and witnessing in clinical practice. *Journal of Analytical Psychology, 43*(2): 239–261.

Wyman-McGinty, W. (2005). Growing a mind: The evolution of thought out of bodily experience. *Spring: A Journal of Archetype and Culture, 72*: 267–279.

Yerushalmi, H. (1999). The roles of group supervision of supervision. *Psychoanalytic Psychology, 16*: 426–447.

Yorke, V. (2005). Bion's vertex as a supervisory object. In: C. Driver & Martin, E. (Eds.). *Supervision and the Analytic Attitude.* pp. 34–49. London: Whurr Publications.

CHAPTER SIX

Supervision of art psychotherapy: transference and countertransference

Elizabeth Rundquist

stablishing a safe holding space, we set the stage for supervision of psychotherapy. Supervisor and supervisee agree to a clear delineation of expectations concerning a particular time frame, fee schedule, policy on payment for missed sessions, and make a secure commitment to the process of supervision. In other words, they establish object constancy as a basis for the healthy growth of the supervisee through the development of her clinical skills and confidence. They develop a trusting relationship for useful exploration of the dynamics of the supervisee/patient dyad as well as the supervisor/supervisee/ patient triad. The supervisor, although not an analyst per se, is nevertheless in direct contact with the supervisee's affects, thoughts, feelings. The supervisee's transferences to the supervisor, and the supervisor's transferences to the supervisee, derived from the early mother/ caregiver imago, are evoked by the power dynamic of the supervisor/ supervisee relationship, and played out in it. Here there is some similarity to the transference–countertransference dialectic in therapy.

Transference is understood as the patient's experience and perception of the analyst as a person who has attributes that evoke feelings similar to those associated with a figure from early childhood. Countertransference can be understood as the analyst's thoughts and feelings that occur in response to receiving these feelings in various situations that are replayed in the analytic setting. Some of these are part of the analyst's objective responses to the patient's dynamics. Others are subjective responses arising from the analyst's own dynamics. It is essential for the patient to recognize the existence not only of the analyst's objective or justified feelings, but also of the analyst's subjective feelings; that is, the analyst must and does develop an unconscious countertransference (Little, 1951, p. 37). Countertransference may become a resistance to knowing and using feelings generated by the patient and to analyzing the infantile roots of conflict. On the other hand, when properly handled, countertransference leads the way to understanding and progress. However, countertransference and transference cannot be so easily separated in practice. In modern thought, "It is the transference–countertransference, not simply the transference, that constitutes the matrix in which psychological meanings are generated in the analytic situation" (Ogden, 1997:47). The whole patient–analyst relationship includes both normal and pathological features, conscious and unconscious elements, transference and countertransference, in varying proportions. It will always include something which is specific to both the individual patient and the individual analyst (Little, 1951, p. 33). Transference–countertransference can be compared to "an observational instrument, an observation platform. On this observational platform the psychoanalyst's task is use himself as a symbolic object that can throw light upon the emotional acts that otherwise remain in darkness" (Symington, 2002, p. 58). In short, transference and countertransference together form the engine driving the therapeutic process whether in psychotherapy or psychoanalysis or in that specialized form of psychotherapy called art therapy.

In art therapy and supervision of art therapists, transference and countertransference are of paramount importance, as they are in psychotherapy and supervision of psychotherapy conducted in the verbal dimension. However, the work of an art therapy supervisor is qualitatively different from that of a supervisor who uses words as the medium of communication. I will describe the role of art media in therapy and supervision. Later in this chapter I will refer to some site visits and to my own creative process as an artist to illustrate various points concerning therapy and supervision that uses art as a medium for self discovery and for growth and development.

The art product does not merely represent a record of activity. It is testimony to something meaningful that took place in a particular time and space between figures of the past and the patient and therapist now. It is an intersubjective object for therapist and patient in treatment. As supervisor and supervise explore the art product it becomes an intersubjective object for them in supervision. It is a creative and esthetic expression that allows emotional discharge and the representation of conscious and unconscious thoughts and feelings and split-off parts of the personality. How the therapist, in this case the art therapist, keeps the frame, establishes a good holding environment, contains and metabolizes primitive affects, and in general makes a "safe" place for the therapeutic work is of crucial importance in the understanding of therapeutic process. The resulting art expression can only be realized in that time and place with those art materials, in response to that therapist-patient dyad, and is further elucidated in supervision as an illuminating object of the patient/therapist/supervisor triad.

In the particular instance of the art therapist supervisee, the art product itself becomes a player, a psychological object, in the session, as an image in real-time, that transfers to the supervisory session. Deri states, "the healthy person is able to create expressive symbolic forms that connect his or her 'inside' with the outside" (Deri, 1988, p. 321). Using the capacity for symbolization as a measure of development, we can think of the art product as a marker of the relative health of the patient. As a tangible object the art becomes a messenger for the essence of the patient. All the anxieties, undreamt thoughts, and feelings experienced in the actual process of making the art can be embodied in the art product.

In supervision, the art product stands in for the patient. The supervision becomes "a combination of the therapeutic relationship and the picture that weaves the therapists into its spell and enchants" (Schaverein, 2007, p. 58). I quote Schaverein at length, as she seems to me best able to describe the real process of working with an image while working in a supervisory relationship. "[I]t is when the therapist conveys the context from which the picture emerged that it becomes animated. Then the supervisor is admitted to the inner frame of the drama of the therapeutic relationship and its atmosphere begins to permeate the supervision" (Schaverein, 2007, p. 58).

Example: early mother/child transference–
countertransference

When I entered the day nursery to meet a young woman intern for whom I was the supervisor, I joined her where she was sitting with small children, gently interacting with them at a small round table. She referred to me as Miss Elizabeth and offered me a seat as though I were an honored guest. I was aware of being a receptacle for the young intern's projections and expectations. I believe in an unconscious way, I represented an idealized primary transference figure. I felt aware of the power I felt in my role as supervisor. It was my job to bring the "knowledge and experience of the supervisor to contain the feelings evoked and the anxieties generated by the clinical material" (Brown, 2007, p. 169). And I would add that I also have to be aware of the anxieties evoked by my presence as a supervisor and observer. At this point my countertransference feelings were useful to me. I remembered my own immaturity, my own over-identifying with my patients, and my feelings of being "one of the kids." As I remembered feeling overwhelmed by responsibility, feeling as though I were working in the dark, I felt for her insecurity. I was aware of wanting to take care of the young intern. I remembered the gratification I had felt when I found an authority to trust. I thought how, as she was quietly taking care of her young charges by her gentle presence, she was perhaps repairing some of her own wishes to have been taken care of.

In this vignette, the defining moment was when I recognized my own past pain and connected it in imagination to hers. I recognized a wish to direct the young intern to therapy. But I was not her caretaker or her therapist. At this moment I felt that I understood the distinction between the role of supervisor and that of therapist with greater clarity. It is not the supervisor's role to provide therapy. It is not the aim of supervision to facilitate deep exploration and interpretation of *sui generis* formations. Yet some supervisees need that degree of exploration and without it they cannot do good therapy. Robbins observed, "problems occur when the student presents with little or no personal therapy and maintains defenses surrounding the projections. A gentle opening up of the topic of transference may facilitate the process. Referral for personal therapy may help in the long run .... [I]n the short run, offering various possible interventions may be the only recourse" (Robbins, 2007:159). Clarity of role, task, and boundary are key. The foremost transference feelings among the young intern, the young charges, and me were all about early mother/child feelings and concomitant underlying dynamics. Empathizing and identifying with the young intern, I was able to tolerate and thus modify my own remembered pain. And, by unconscious containment, modify the young intern's feelings.

Example: independence, dependence, transference/ countertransference

I was visiting a locked in-patient behavioral unit where I was to meet with an intern whose task it was to provide a safe space for conducting an art therapy group. Observing her at work were three observers: the on-site supervisor, a social work intern, and me, the visiting supervisor. The intern provided safe space and "held" the group (Winnicott, 1971, p. 150). She skillfully elicited thoughts and feelings around the art created in the session, facilitated heretofore unexpressed affects in response to the art, fostered reflection, and detoxified feelings.

My visit to this in inpatient psychiatric unit in an old river town, evoked in me feelings of dread, feelings of getting lost in the poor, run-down streets, and memories of my own experience as an intern in a locked psychiatric unit in another old neighborhood in another old city. At a deeper level, fears of going back into the violent, troublesome past were evoked. Miracle of miracles, the art therapy intern, openly mentioned her nervousness at being observed. I reassured her that feeling nervous was to be expected. Aware of my own fear, coming from a different or perhaps the same place of anxiety, I was able to address my supervisee's underlying issue head-on. Searles describes owning one's conflicts "as a humanizing effort, particularly in psychiatric units" (Searles, 1988, p. 345). In the above instance, she, as supervisee, and I, as supervisor, were each feeling anxious. I learned later that she had called her husband about her nervousness, and that when she had seen me the nervousness went away. The simple act of humanizing and normalizing the experience had the powerful effect of relieving her anxiety and mine. The example points to the "enormous responsibility to be the recipient of such idealized transferences. It is illustrative of power relations" (Case, 2007:109). The risk is that speaking words of reassurance will encourage dependence on the supervisor. Then how does the supervisor encourage independence? By consciously adopting a reflective, observing stance, and thinking with the supervisee about what had just happened, the supervisor can provide a counterpoint to the overwhelming experience. Together, supervisor and supervisee can discharge tension, and use transference feelings to intuit and metabolize the experience.

Observing the group at work making art, I noticed that the patients seemed transfixed and engrossed in their task, seemingly oblivious to the three health-care workers in the room. It was as if they were in a dream. "To the extent that one is capable of dreaming one's experience, one is able to generate an emotional response to it, learn from, and be changed by it" (Ogden, 2005, p. 23). Making art connects the patients to the dream space, a place of creativity and recovery. A painting is a visual image, existing in time and space. However, like a night dream, a painting reflects the dream state of the dreamer as artist. Naturally, the making of an art product also entails cognitive functioning, skill, and decision making. Nevertheless, the actual state of creating is dreamlike in that a visual image expresses the fusion of conscious and unconscious states. To illustrate my meaning of entering the dream state, I will now describe my own creative process as a painter.

Example: the artist's creative process

Before I actually paint, I mix colors, while thinking about value, tone, and composition. The act of thinking, mixing, and developing a palette, leads to associations that flit through my consciousness. When I actually begin to put brush to canvas, I am in something like a dream state. During the actual process of wielding the bush, I am certainly conscious of where I am; yet, my mind and body are engaged in a trance-like dance. Often, I apply paint to the canvas, quickly moving from one area to another, stopping to mix more colors, checking the impact, free associating, choosing the placement of pigment, building up composition, unaware of anything else, fully engaged in expressing unexplored, previously unplumbed thoughts, with color as the catalyst. It all comes together in a product that is concerned with space, volume, line, and color, and then "it says something." It is at this point, I, as the artist, can see what I have painted. I reflect on it and understand what the image represents in my life.

On one occasion, I experienced a cathartic release of feelings I had experienced witnessing a spectacular summer rainstorm viewed from a balcony overlooking a mountain range. The resulting image on the canvas was not representational at all, but conveyed a feeling of awe, perhaps wonder, remembrance of past summer rain storms, and myriad unexpressed thoughts, including gratitude for the privilege of being alive. Does the viewer see this? I don't know, but I, as the painter, can use my painting to reflect upon and realize my un-thought dream. The residue of the day, the experience of the past, informs the night-time dreaming of the sleeper and the waking dreaming of the artist. We dream, rewinding the events of the day, connecting with unacknowledged and un-thought feelings, and hopefully working out problems. The art product, in contrast to the night-time dream that remains ephemeral, enters into the real world, visible for people other than the dreamer to see and experience.

Returning to the example

As for the intern in the locked psychiatric unit, I like to think she felt held and contained as we observed her, and that she was then able to contain and hold the patients, allowing them to be alone in the company of others. She held open a safe space for the group. At work, they seemed oblivious to the onlookers, lost in a dream. But the dream was made manifest in their art. As she led the patients skillfully to explore their work, they were able to think and give form to previously unexpressed and un-thought feeling states. The patients felt empowered by her provision of a good creative experience, the intern felt empowered to work well with them, and all of them were showing growth towards independence. My countertransference was a feeling of happiness at a job well done by all.

The impact of gender, class, geographical location, and race on culture

Historically, in the West, those in power have been white. "[L]anguage has been used by those in power to inculcate at an unconscious level, a sense that black is negative and inferior, and the reason for this is to create a division between 'the haves, and must not haves'" (Dalley qtd in Skaife, 2007, p. 140). The same can be said of gender, class, country, state, or even town of origin as determinants of our experience of our culture. How do supervisors cope with all of this? They do so by being aware, developing perspective on the impact of these aspects, seeing our shared humanity, undergoing their own therapy to work toward clarification of conscious and unconscious biases.

Example: awareness of being white

I went to make a site visit to a Wellness Center in a down-at-the-heels town, aware of some conscious bias and a host of countertransference feelings. The Center, an attractively decorated haven in a makeshift building, provides counseling, art therapy, and a safe place for teens at risk, and those already affected by substance abuse, remanded by the court for state mandated care of minors, and fetal alcohol syndrome survivors. The intern and I, the visiting supervisor, were the only ones there with white skin. We were a minority within a minority, aware that the culture in the West has given the white-skinned person the author- ity to be the mover of the game. In this instance, all was seemingly reversed. Politeness ruled, yet I experienced an unspoken undercurrent of their feeling as if they were saying, "This is our place! We have made it out of whatever we had at hand, and we are very proud. Don't come here and try to lord it over us. We won't let you." None of this was actu- ally spoken, but I, the visiting supervisor, in reaction to this feeling and in an attempt to reassure them and me, was perhaps overly friendly, condescendingly making myself humble in the face of overwhelming feelings of guilt at my sense of white privilege.

The on-site supervisor seemed well aware of her power, as she sat behind a desk in a large swivel chair, while the intern and I sat at her feet, so to speak, in smaller chairs. The physical evidence of power, culture, identity, yours and mine, each carrying different colors and histories, was objectively conveyed and subjectively felt. Instead of embracing the difference, our culture exaggerates it, weights it to the white side, and creates dysfunction. The white-skinned intern was ele- vated to a position of power: "Let them see what good mothering is. You are modeling the good mother for these at risk kids." The idea that the white-skinned culture at large is the repository of good mothering reflects an inversion of power, as though good mothering was inher- ently white.

How does the supervisor navigate such a tricky minefield? I think, again, by exploring her own transference projections, reflecting on her countertransference feelings, and understanding her cultural biases. For instance, in the example of supervising at the Wellness Center for at risk teens, I was aware of feelings of shame at my narcissistically perceived superiority. Acknowledging my shameful feelings brought me to a place of inferiority, and to a more human place. Perhaps we all were feeling our own versions of superiority and inferiority. We experienced feelings of power and powerlessness and anger at a system so filled with injustice, historical inequity, and the pitting of different groups over and against one another. What seemed to me to be the most important characteristic of the Wellness Center was its refusal to confirm cultural expectations of its being one one-down and impotent.

Our own conflicts are of use and are not to be dismissed (Searles, H., 1955, p. 47). No one is completely free of bias, impulses, and vulnerabilities. It is our job as supervisors to know our biases, our cultural determinants and social history, and the meaning of our impulses so that they do not lead to false judgments and destructive actions. As supervisors, we are in a position of authority. Respecting that, not abusing power, and recognizing its impact on our supervisees enables us to help them with their issues of authority in their work with patients and institutions. We create a safe place where uncomfortable feelings such as inadequacy and shame can be expressed, so that our supervisees can accept the troublesome aspects of our culture, and the part each of us plays within it.

Example

My next supervisory visit took place in a well-funded family treatment center with well-equipped consulting rooms. I was there to work with Jerry, an art therapy intern. Jerry was courtly as he introduced me to his site director, Helen, an affable, agreeable woman with penetrating eyes and a cordial manner that made me feel welcome. Helen's large corner office was filled with all sorts of objects, including a sculpture of a silver head with two large watch-faces as eyes. Her power and status were apparent. I felt I was in the presence of another personage. Yet she had a sense of the absurd. I felt a kinship, and I liked her. I felt in touch with my own power too as we talked about Freud and object relations. Thinking and reflecting about contemporary thought gave us something in common. Jerry was taking it all in. He told me that the session coming up was with SandPlay. I said that I was happy to hear that and eager to learn, never having seen SandPlay in action. Helen said it was fantastic, and so they had bought the whole system.

Jerry took me down the hall to the consulting room, and went to get Laurence, an intelligent-looking 9-year-old boy, diagnosed with ADHD. Jerry had previously cleared it with Laurence that I would be observing this session. Laurence wore thick glasses and a trapper hat, which he would keep on for the whole session, as if he wanted to hide. When Jerry introduced me to him, Laurence politely said "Hi", without looking up. Jerry and I both asked Laurence if it was all right for me to sit down, and he, pointing to a chair close to the SandPlay box, said I could sit there. I felt as though I were waiting for the curtain to go up, for the play to begin. I felt like a child out for a treat.

Jerry gave Laurence many baskets, filled with small objects. Laurence took his time choosing characters, monsters, cars, and trucks. Soon the sand tray was filled with 30 or so figures, all destined for some sort of role, each one with the potential to represent some aspect of Laurence's inner world. Jerry and Laurence seemed to be quite content with each other. I saw a good therapeutic alliance there. I felt like an observer, not part of the interaction, and I noticed that a figure that might represent me was pushed to the side of the field of play. Jerry was quietly mirroring Laurence's comments. As time progressed, Laurence's voice became more agitated, his play more violent. Finally, the huge, many-tentacled gorgon-eyed monster was let out of the corner, attacking others seemingly randomly, making loud sounds. Laurence became very directive, attempting to pull me into the fray, and telling me that I was there to hit Jerry. I wondered what I might be projecting that Laurence would think that of me; or perhaps, he was projecting his primary negative transference on to me, as indicated by making that figure stand apart, the one I thought might represent me. I said nothing, keeping the frame, while observing Jerry closely leaning in over the sand tray, appearing to protect Laurence. As the session continued, Laurence transformed the figure that I thought was me into a good object to take care of Jerry who had been felled by the monster.

At one point, close to the end of the session, Laurence wanted his dad to come in. Jerry let the subject lie low for a while. Again Laurence voiced his wish for his dad to come in. Jerry turned to me and asked me, "What do you think?" I looked at Jerry, not wanting to either rescue him or deprive him of his own power to think and act, and turned the question back to him, saying, "What do you think?" Jerry replied, "I'm ambivalent about it." I did not reply. Laurence kept on working, saying that all the monsters are out. Jerry did not call the dad in at that point, but five minutes or so later he asked Laurence if it was now time for dad to come in. Laurence said yes.

My role was to provide a holding place for both Jerry and Laurence and to share my observations with Jerry after the session was over. Not in direct language but in play, Laurence was expressing angry feelings perhaps because I had intruded on his time alone with Jerry and because although I was allowed in, his father was not. The sequences of events—the setting, the introductions, the respect for the child, the relationship between therapist and child, the impact of the observer, the feelings made manifest in various roles in play—illustrate the forms of authority expressed in various roles and the power of maintaining the frame to provide a safe holding space for uncomfortable feelings.

As the supervisor I was well aware of the authority given to me and the power of my ability to contain my responses without action and speech. I did not rescue, in order to allow uncomfortable feelings develop, and I could wait until later to give voice to those feelings that Jerry and Laurence could not verbalize. As the supervisee realizes that he will not weaken and crumble, he grows in confidence and skill. In this hierarchical system the ultimate beneficiary of power emanating from Helen, the director and Jerry, the intern, is Laurence, the young patient, who is learning to tolerate his murderous rage, and own his good object feelings. Laurence's trust in the protection and strength offered by his therapist allowed him to express angry feelings that were both exciting and frightening. At a later time, Jerry would help Laurence express his angry feelings verbally, as Jerry would become more attuned to his own feelings, and less afraid of his own anger at being observed by a supervisor.

I was moved at Laurence's trust, at his eagerness to enter in to the imaginative arena offered by Jerry and the SandPlay tray, at the illuminating nature of the SandPlay session, and at the environment of the center that so fully valued imagination. Ultimately the art therapy encounter, given voice in the supervisory setting can give birth to possibilities that did not exist in time and space before.

As supervisees we are dependent on our supervisors to provide a non-judgmental space in which to process our transference/counter transference issues. We may hate the dependence, yet need the holding. We may love our dependence and find it gratifying. It is useful to understand that the love and the hatred derive from earlier dependency needs. Our independence is hard earned. As graduate licensed psychotherapists we still seek supervision from time to time so that we do not split off toxic feelings that can lead to burn out if not processed. This impels us to accept our limits and take in the learning from our supervisor. To offer and receive supervision is an aspect of our professional responsibility.

References

Brown, C., Meyerowitz-Katz, J. & Ryde, J. (2007). Thinking with image making. Supervising with image making. In: J. Schaverien, & C. Case (Eds.), *Supervision of Art Psychotherapy: A theoretical and practical handbook* (pp. 167–181). London and New York: Routledge.

Case, C. (2007). Imagery in supervision: The non-verbal narrative of knowing. In: J. Schaverien, & C. Case (Eds.), *Supervision of Art Psychotherapy: A theoretical and practical handbook*. pp. 95–115. London and New York: Routledge.

Deri, S. (1984). Fostering good symbolization. In: *Creativity and Symbolization*. pp. 320–324. Madison, CT: International Universities Press, Inc.

Little, M. (1951). Counter-transference and the patient's response to it. *International Journal of Psycho-Analysis, 32*: 32–40.

Ogden, T. H. (2005). This art of psychoanalysis: dreaming undreamt dreams and interrupted cries. In: *This Art of Psychoanalysis: Dreaming undreamt dreams and interrupted cries*. pp. 1–18. USA and Canada: Routledge.

Robbins, A. (2007). The art of supervision. In: J. Schaverien, & C. Case (Eds.), *Supervision of Art Psychotherapy A theoretical and practical handbook*. pp. 153–166. London and New York: Routledge.

Skaife, S. (2007). Working in black and white: an art therapy supervision group. *Supervision of Art Psychotherapy A theoretical and practical handbook*. pp. 139–152. London and New York: Routledge.

Schaverien, J. & Case, C (Eds.) (2007). *Supervision of Art Psychotherapy A theoretical and practical handbook*. London and New York: Routledge.

Searles, H. F. (1955). Dependency processes in the psychotherapy of schizophrenia. *Journal of the American Psychoanalytic Association, 3*: 19–66. Retrieved from http: www.pepweb.com.

Symington, N. (2002). Emotional action. In: *A Pattern of Madness*. pp. 56–63. London and New York: Karnac.

Winnicott, D. W. (1971). *Playing and Reality*. USA and Canada: Routledge.

CHAPTER SEVEN

Social workers' experience of conflict in psychotherapy supervision

Elizabeth H. Thomas

I am by training and practice a clinical social worker and a psychotherapist. I have always had a special interest in the role of supervision in the professional development of clinical social workers. The impetus for my study came out of this personal interest, the centrality of supervision for psychotherapy training, the ubiquitous nature of conflict in human relations, and the promising perspective of the supervisee. All of these factors relate to the clinical social worker's responsibility to serve well the patient in psychotherapy. I wanted to advance understanding of the specific phenomenon of conflict that many of us have experienced in supervision, and thereby to improve the design of supervision so that it is more beneficial to the supervisee and, by extension, to the patient. I found that conflict in supervision coalesced around issues of power, trust, and the process of learning. In this chapter I will present the methodology of the study, consider the findings and their contribution to the practice of supervision, and consider their relevance to clinical social work and society at large. I will critique my research methods and procedures, look at the results of my study in relation to literature on supervision, and make recommendations for future studies. I will conclude with a narrative of the impact of this study on my personal and professional life.

The qualitative, phenomenological approach
with triangulation

The research that I designed and conducted was a qualitative study focused on the basic question, "What is the experience of conflict in supervision?" I used a phenomenological approach, a departure from previous research designs used to study this aspect of psychotherapy supervision (Creswell, 1998; Padgett, 1998; Patton, 2002). The purpose of phenomenological research is to elucidate the essence or meaning of human experience through qualitative descriptions. The method provides a systematic, disciplined, and critical process for derivation of knowledge. The particular methodology employed in this study is based on the transcendental phenomenology of Edmund Husserl (1859–1938), a German philosopher and mathematician. Phenomenological methodology most often seeks data through face-to-face interviews. Interviewing is a logical strategy for data collection since "participants of a process are in the best position to reflect on it" (Ely & Matias, 2001, p. 1; also see Bruner, 1990; Lincoln & Guba, 1985; Mishler, 1986). This seemingly obvious conclusion is echoed by Stimmel (1995) who states simply, "Perhaps the best place for a teacher to go to learn how to teach is to his or her students" (p. 615).

This question, "What is the experience of conflict in supervision?" was the starting point for in depth interviews with clinical social worker supervisees (the co-researchers) about their experience in supervision. The interviews were transcribed and analyzed. Nine co-researchers were interviewed for this study. All were female, and all had completed formal training in social work through the Masters level. The co-researchers' ages ranged from 28 to 61; their years in licensed practice ranged from one to 16. Eight of the nine interviews addressed the subject of conflict in supervision and, thus, were relevant to the research question. One interview addressed conflict outside of the supervision experience and, therefore, was discarded. All of the experiences reported took place while the participant was enrolled in or contemplating advanced training, or while working in an agency setting. The supervisors were mainly social workers except for one, who was a psychiatrist/psychoanalyst. Six of the supervisors were female, two were male.

To support verification of the data received in the interviews, I secured from each interviewee two written self-report questionnaires related to the experience of the supervision just discussed in the interview. *The Supervisory Styles Inventory* (Friedlander & Ward, 1984) uses three sub-scales to assess the trainee's perception of the supervisor's style. The sub-scales are reliable (Cronbach's alpha ranging from .76 to .93) and valid predictors of trainee's satisfaction with supervision, supervisor's theoretical orientation, and trainee experience level. *The Role Conflict and Role Ambiguity Inventory* (Olk & Friedlander, 1992) addresses the degree of conflict/ambiguity operating in respondents' experience. This instrument uses two sub-scales that are reliable (Cronbach's alpha of .89 for role conflict and .91 for role ambiguity) and predictive of work-related anxiety, dissatisfaction with supervision, and general work dissatisfaction.

I gave these questionnaires to participants at the conclusion of the research interview, along with a self-addressed, stamped envelope, and asked them to complete the questionnaires and return them to me within one week. In order to maintain anonymity of the respondents, I coded the responses to correspond to the coded tape transcriptions. I arranged to corroborate the data by triangulation, viewing it from three points (1 narrative and 2 questionnaires) a standard feature of the phenomenological approach. According to Padgett (1998), triangulation is "the convergence of multiple perspectives that can provide greater confidence that what is being targeted is being accurately captured" (p. 32). Schwandt (1997) notes, "Triangulation is a means of checking the integrity of the inferences one draws" (p. 163). Since use of the questionnaires were solely for purposes of corroboration, their data are relevant only in relation to the corresponding interviews. They were not intended to provide data to be compared across subjects. To further support the validity of the data, I relied on *rich, thick description* (extensive, detailed, word-for-word narratives of each interview and its emotional and cognitive impact), *peer review* of the data and *member checks* (discussion among my peer cohort of PhD candidates), and *clarification of researcher bias* (in discussion with my PhD advisers and my peer group).

Contributions and implications of the study

I wanted to understand the experience of conflict in supervision for the purpose of advancing understanding of this phenomenon and learning how best to structure supervision so that it is beneficial to the supervisee. Further, with improved circumstances for supervision and a better understanding of the factors that play a part in conflict, the experience can be one that benefits not only the supervisee, but also the supervisor and the patient.

The task was one of looking for those constituents of the experience of conflict in supervision that were invariant for each co-researcher and across co-researchers. These invariant constituents are what comprise the meaning structure of conflict in supervision. I found that these invariant constituents are *power, trust, and learning*. These essential findings, and the experience they represent, offer insight into other elements of the supervisory experience and suggest tenets necessary for supervision to be a satisfying and productive experience. They are as follows:

- a good working alliance is essential;
- mutuality and respect strengthen the working alliance;
- clarity of role facilitates the task;
- if power is exploited, the consequences can be dire;
- trust languishes in the face of power abuses;
- learning depends on an open mind that is unencumbered by fear;
- losses are never eradicated, only integrated over time;
- one's experience is the arbiter of what is true.

This study and the literature reviewed

Supervision is a relational endeavor, and the quality of the relationship is a predictor of outcome. When the relationship between supervisor and supervisee is positive, and there is a working alliance, then the supervision is likely to be beneficial to the supervisee and, presumably, to the patient. When there is unresolved conflict in the supervisory relationship, the endeavor falters and fails.

Studies on good or successful supervision show a positive relationship between supervisees' positive ratings and supervisors who attend to the person and concerns of the supervisee. Empathy and attunement on the part of the supervisor are key qualities in the assessment of "excellence" in supervision (Shanfield et al., 1992, 1993). This study looked to the negative side of the supervisory relationship and the occurrence of conflict. By their absence, findings would underscore the importance of attunement and mutuality. It is by the absence of empathy and understanding of the supervisee's concerns in those supervisions characterized by conflict that it is presumed that the presence of these factors would support an experience of good supervision.

The research by Nelson and Friedlander (2001) on problematic supervision identified power struggles and dual relationships as primary themes. Their study also drew attention to role conflict as a salient factor for experienced supervisees, who felt disappointment and resentment when the expected collegiality is missing from the supervisory relationship. The findings of my study generally support those of Nelson and Friedlander. My results were the same as theirs regarding four issues:

1. the power differential in supervision is a key factor in the experience of conflict;
2. trust is a casualty in relationships that rupture and are left unrestored;
3. the experience of supervisees' development of coping strategies can be reparative and contributes to resolution within the self;
4. a good supervisory relationship is at the heart of good supervision. This last shared finding comes by inference and is supported by research on good supervision (Shanfield et al., 1992, 1993; Worthen & McNeill, 1996).

My study did not develop the theme of dual relationships that was a major finding for Nelson and Friedlander because it was not designed to do so and is, therefore, neutral on this issue, neither supporting nor discrediting the importance of dual relationships when there is conflict in supervision. Future research would usefully serve the question by examining this aspect of the supervisory relationship.

Three findings that distinguish my study from previous research

1) Loss of learning opportunity

First, when there is conflict in supervision for the supervisee, a central theme revolves around issues of learning and lost opportunity. Here there are profound emotional and psychological dimensions of experience for the supervisee, having to do with both personal and professional identity, as well as with expectations that contrast with the disappointments inherent in reality. The experience of learning lost speaks to the primitive neural function that allocates cognitive resources and directs energy to tasks of survival and self-protection in the face of danger. The supervisee who feels threatened in supervision is not wholly available to learn in that moment. The supervisees interviewed in this study were often able to appreciate their supervisor's instruction upon reflection, but not at the time. The supervisees recognized that while in the midst of the conflict, they were not able to learn. If there was learning from the engagement with the supervisor it was only after the fact.

Another dimension to the loss of learning is the deep disappointment experienced by the supervisees interviewed. The depth of disappointment was striking, especially given that most of those interviewed had had previous supervisions, which would suggest that the emergence of conflict might be anticipated, at least in the abstract. But the disappointment, resentment, anger, and sadness that was engendered suggest that these losses reached psychic depths, of coming to know the reality versus the ideal. Coming to know hard reality functioned to demythologize the idealized supervisor.

2) Level of detail

Secondly, it is the detail of this study that distinguishes it from previous research, including the qualitative study of Nelson and Friedlander. Phenomenological studies represent ground level research, the foundation for further investigations into a subject. Here, the rich detail stands out in providing a true starting point for future research studies on conflict in supervision. This is evident in the final stages of the method in which themes and essences are elaborated as to texture and structure. The result is an understanding of an experience that can only come from living inside of it. The difference is in the power of the narrative.

3) Emotional depth

Finally, it is worth noting that the in-depth interview functioned in an unanticipated way to benefit both the researcher and the interviewee. As an interviewer, the researcher's stance was one of an interested listener, who sought detail and clarity. The interview supplied the researcher with data, but it also provided the interviewee with an occasion to reflect on an unpleasant experience and to advance integration of the experience. The interviews took place at a time and in a place largely determined by the participant. These two factors helped establish a setting where the interviewee might proceed in her quest for resolution.

Because the topic specifically focused on conflict, discussion drew from deeper troughs that had been visited infrequently, if at all. The interviewees came to the project having put conflicted experiences aside, often for years, because it had left a bitter taste. Had I been inquiring about positive supervisory experiences, the data may have come more easily and from a more accessible place. The interview itself provided the interviewees with an opportunity to revisit and rework a conflict that had impacted the interviewees personally and professionally. So, the one being interviewed often felt relief and affirmation as she told the story of her experience. The effect was clearer thinking and enhanced reflection. Thus, the interview process seemed to have served a therapeutic purpose and had a reparative effect.

An interview that illustrates loss of learning, level of detail, and emotional depth

The co-researcher being interviewed had enrolled in a training program after some time away from the field of social work. She spoke hesitantly, questioningly, and associatively about a conflict she experienced as an insecure beginner, describing her memory of what occurred in supervision, revisiting the pain of it, and looking at her responsibility for how her supervisor interpreted the supervisory task. The following extracts were selected from her interview data. Even with pauses, repetitions, and graphic material from the raw data essential to my research now edited out for ease of reading, the quotes illustrate the emotional depth, level of detail in the narrative, and loss of the learning opportunity. Even so, the co-researcher salvaged important learning about how supervision should be conducted.

> "What happened was that I feel like things, the boundaries got a
> little blurred. My supervisor shared information about his own life,
> and then would say things like, oh my gosh, I can't believe I told
> you that, I haven't told anybody that, but that's sort of a secret. So
> he'd want me to keep a secret for him, kind of thing. One time he
> wanted me to go with him to pay his cleaning person at his house,

go to the bank, the bookstore, various places. And at that point I did say, you know, I will do this but I am not going to pay for this supervision."

The co-researcher notices the loss of learning opportunity

"He would be late, always sort of late. I was very big on being on time. … He would answer phone calls from family members during our supervision … . Then there felt to me that there was a very flirtatious piece to this supervision—and, again, I thought how much did I play, am I responsible?

"Right from the beginning there was an aspect of this supervision which was sort of exciting like I was feeling like, wow, I am getting this big guy that's funny and, you know, and I did feel like there was something special about me because I did feel like he was interested in me and whatever … . There were sort of some uncomfortable feelings of something not being quite right, and some pressure, but nothing really happened.

"He would say, well, don't tell me that you're not aware of some feelings between us. But I wasn't willing to address that with him. And that it was up for me to deal with on my own in some way … . Now, I would be clear. At the time, I simply said, no, I am not aware of that."

The co-researcher continues to share the blame and recognizes her wish to empathize with and protect her supervisor

"There is a sense of how much did I play into it? Is it right for me to be blaming him? I'm not exactly fully blaming him …. Obviously I'm not mentioning his name, whatever, and this is not going to go anywhere. I am sort of protecting him in the sense that I am feeling like I am required to hold the secret, for instance, that he shared with me. There was a secret about his own personal life and about—clearly indicating that he was having some problems. So he was going through a difficult time.

"I was a little too loosey-goosey in terms of my talking and whatever, which I tend to be, so I must be responsible. It didn't happen with the other person, and all. I can't get to the point of, how dare he do that! I mean that was really unfair to me!"

Having revisited the conflict, by the close of the interview, the co-researcher can reflect back on the conflict from a position of greater security as a professional

> "I do look back and sort of feel like it is the job of the supervisor to be the one to absolutely keep the boundaries, okay? I mean, intellectually that's very clear. It's a situation where the power is unequal. It would be less unequal now because I would be more a part of the profession and feeling I know myself and I wouldn't feel as unequal. It felt very unequal power wise. Now, there wouldn't be anybody that would really be able to make me feel sort of intimidated. That just wouldn't happen."

The co-researcher begins to see the difference between her preference for a loose style of relating and the need for firm boundaries—she understands the impact of the power differential

> "I think in the past I tended to be, as I still am in part, a little free floating and sort of connect well with people who do it the same way, but also feel like there has to be clarity. There can be flexibility, but also really clear boundaries within which the flexibility is. I think it is important to keep in mind that there is going to be a difference from the beginning in the power and that that affects everything. It isn't two friends."

This study and the literature on relational theory literature

A major finding of this study is that relational factors in the supervisory dyad have a profound impact not only on the course of the supervision, but on the integrity of the entire supervisory enterprise. The relationship between supervisor and supervisee is a fundamental determinant of the quality and usefulness of the supervision. The literature suggests this to be the case, and the current study supports this finding as well. It is in line with the findings of this study, and encouraging as well, that several volumes have been published in recent years placing relational factors at the heart of supervision (Bernard & Goodyear, 1998; Frawley-O'Dea, & Sarnat, 2001; Kaiser, 1997).

As noted in the original literature review for this study, the fundamental role of supervision in the development of social work clinicians is a pedagogical imperative to examine what occurs in the supervisory relationship and to determine the factors that contribute to the development of clinical skill. The fact that conflict emerges in supervision is not surprising. However, the manner in which conflict is managed and resolved will impact the therapist in training and ultimately the welfare of the client. Thus, it is the relationship represented in the supervisory dyad that holds the key to how and whether conflict is addressed, resolved, and ultimately used for growth and development of the supervisee, and thereby the patient. The quality of the supervisory relationship is a vital determinant in the efficacy of supervision. The conceptual lens of relational theory, as evolved from the ideas of self psychology and interpersonal theory, is helpful in conceptualizing how to conduct clinical supervision effectively. A tenet of self psychology is to focus on the subjective experience of both the therapist and the patient. Similarly in supervision, empathic attunement between supervisor and supervisee is the model, rather than a focus on proper technique or referral of countertransference reactions to one's therapist or analyst for illumination outside the supervision. Within an optimal responsiveness model, the supervisee is less likely to feel threatened and more likely to have a sense of safety and affirmation in the supervision.

Relational theory that could apply in supervision

Bacal (1998) emphasizes the concept of "optimal responsiveness" in the therapeutic encounter as a reciprocal responsibility that is shared by a particular therapist and a particular patient that is therapeutically relevant and timely for the patient. Kindler (1998) references Bacal's therapeutic ideal of optimal responsiveness, applies it to psychotherapy supervision, and maintains that the supervisory relationship is one wherein the supervisor and the supervisee function with and for each other as selfobjects. This interrelationship and mutual interaction echoes that of Winnicott's baby and mother dyad. Wolf (1988) joins the selfobject functions in supervision by pointing out that psychic structure emerges in development and in the process of therapy. Similarly, in the supervisory situation, the sense of self comes to include the self as clinician. Similar to the experience of supervisees in the current study, Schindelheim (1995) writes from the perspective of the supervisee and conveys the vulnerability of the supervisee in the relationship. But unlike the experience of participants in this study, where there was no resolution with the supervisor, the disruption he describes at the beginning of his supervision with Evelyn Schwaber was repaired through mutual efforts by both supervisor and supervisee to understand the needs and vulnerabilities of each. Frawley-O'Dea and Sarnat (2001) take a constructivist view of the treatment relationship, wherein therapist and patient enact and explicate the internalized world of the patient, and expand it to include the supervisory dyad. Working within a relational matrix that includes patient, therapist/supervisee, and supervisor, the patient's narrative is co-constructed and potentiality for all three is enlarged. "Through the two dyad's ever more complete delineation of the … relationship, mediated in part through increasingly deeper and wider elaboration of the supervisory relationship, more becomes possible" (p. 69).

This relational paradigm, with emphasis on mutuality and negotiation in supervision, contributes to the professional development of the supervisee. It seeks to bring to the supervisory experience the message being taught in the supervision of the patient and the therapy. That is, relationship and experience are transformative. Thus, contemporary constructivist views offer potential not only to the therapeutic endeavor but also to the supervisory enterprise. A relational paradigm, that seeks openness and mutuality, holds tremendous potential to enlighten the supervisee's experience of conflict in supervision, and offers a conceptual framework supported by the findings of this study. Such an approach brings together three elements that grounded this study, all related in purpose and process: 1) the researcher's interest in the human experience of a particular event, 2) inquiry into and rich description of that experience, and 3) location of such experience within a relational matrix by constructivist process.

Social and professional implications of my findings

Conflict frequently manifests in the home, the workplace, and the social surround of one's daily life. It is a rare day that passes without any expression of conflict, even if just in the form of a simple misunderstanding. On a larger, more ominous scale, conflict threatens international relations and the strength of the world community. In the educative and developmental interests of clinical supervision, conflict has consequences, as this study has demonstrated. But the implications for social work reach beyond the supervisory dyad per se and into the pedagogical responsibilities and programs of the social work profession in general and beyond it to society in general.

Implications for social work

It is to be hoped that most experiences of supervision are positive and advance the supervisee's professional development. The particulars of successful supervision have been the subject of other studies (Worthen & McNeill, 1996). Supervision that goes awry is troublesome and worthy of investigation, and this study has attempted to make a contribution in this regard. How conflict can be productively managed depends on the willingness of both parties to address problems as they come up. Given this premise, it would seem advisable that supervisor and supervisee discuss from the beginning the expectations and parameters of the particular supervision so that misunderstandings can be corrected and objectives clarified. Some have even recommended that supervisory contracts be drafted and agreed to in the beginning (Bernard & Goodyear, 1998; Kaiser, 1997).

It may be that conflict emerges out of apprehension and insecurity on the part of both parties, supervisor and supervisee, and that defensiveness accrues as insecurities are cultivated. Even though this study did not investigate the experience of the supervisor, Frawley-O'Dea and Sarnat (2001) note that the supervisor is not necessarily the culprit in incidents of conflict. Rather, the supervisor, being human too, may come to the supervision with his or her own burdens, for instance, "the supervisor's pull to think conceptually about clinical material can be understood as a defensive adaptation to the impoverished and contaminated database from which the supervisor operates. It is our way of not feeling stupid when we are confronted with a very difficult and confusing task" (p. 78). Supervisors do not have it so easy.

Just as the brilliant mathematician may be a disaster as a teacher, so too the gifted therapist may make a poor supervisor. One's professional designation does not in and of itself qualify one to teach the craft. Too often good therapists are recruited to supervise, and they are ill prepared. While therapy and supervision are similar, they are sufficiently different that care ought to be taken to ensure the effective function of each. One example from this research involved the supervisor's position of abstinence. The supervisor used a psychoanalytic technique in use to assist progress in analysis by avoiding gratification of patient transference wishes (Moore & Fine, 1990). While abstinence on the part of the therapist may advance the progress of therapy, the benefits of such a stance in supervision seem negligible, if any. Formal training in supervision seems an obvious recommendation, but one that remains neglected in many training programs and agencies.

Criteria for appointment of clinical supervisors ought to extend beyond issues of availability, seniority, or credentials (Veach, 2001). Furthermore, it would seem judicious for training programs to assign supervisees to supervisors who have examined their own interpersonal dynamics through psychotherapy, who have had formal training in supervision, and who have completed a screening process before being offered the responsibility of supervising therapists in training.

One of the age-old axioms of social work is "begin where the client is." This is sage advice, offered in the social worker's very first efforts to treat a troubled client, often in the first year of social work school. It is wise counsel usefully recalled by social workers over and over again, even after many years of practice. Based on the results of this study, supervisors might appropriate this advice and apply it to working with the supervisee; namely, "begin where the supervisee is."

Implications for society

Because conflict is ubiquitous, understanding the processes and constituents of the supervision is useful for every human encounter. The one-on-one contact at the center of this study provides the format for multiple interpersonal relationships, such as between neighbors, spouses, merchant and customer, between an administrative director and his or her staff, to name a few. Or it may be a familial setting of brother and sister, or stepparent and child, or the whole family, intact and extended, in the context of an important event, such as a graduation or wedding.

The lessons of this study can inform the realm of human relationship from supervisory dyads to international affairs. This is an optimistic study, the results of which can be applied in the interest of positive, not destructive relations. Knowing what goes wrong in an interaction is one of the ways to correct the problem before it is full-blown and beyond repair, whether in supervision, in the neighborhood advisory meeting, or in strategic preparations for war. The circumference is ever widening in the pool of human relationship and interaction. Even the outer reaches of human relations on the scale of international relations between countries can be rife with conflict, even when nations have historically been allies. Understanding at this level is as important, if not more so, as that considered in the study at hand.

Limitations of this study and future research

This study suggests several directions in which future research might productively go. The circumstance of dual relationships provides an interesting and useful topic for future exploration. A study of conflict that seeks data from both members of the supervisory dyad would elucidate better the interpersonal process through which conflict develops. Further investigation of developmental variance would help in planning supervision for trainees at different stages of clinical experience.

My study was not designed to ascertain the significance of differences in gender and culture that emerge in the supervisory dyad, though curiosity was heightened when these differences showed up in the supervisee's experience. Useful information would come from research into these areas of difference. Regarding gender, data in this study was confined to the experience of female supervisees. This resulted as a happenstance of the sampling method and the demographics of the profession of social work, which is disproportionately represented by women. Thus, the study is limited by gender. Other areas of differences within the dyad that lend themselves to investigation, in addition to gender and culture, include level of experience, theoretical orientation, and style.

This study focused on individual supervision. It could be surmised that the experience of conflict in group supervision would yield different data, as, for one thing, secrecy would not be as great a factor and, for another, groups, by definition, provide witnesses. The dynamics would likely be very different. An examination of conflict in this setting would be very informative for understanding the factors and processes involved when conflict develops in supervision.

Yet other areas of interest include studies that examine the occurrence and operation of prejudice and discrimination in supervision. The field would benefit from additional studies that identify the qualities of "good enough" supervision. And future research would be strengthened by ongoing observational methods.

The most important motivation for any study of the supervisory or treatment process is the welfare of and potential benefit to the patient. Studies that examine the extent and nature of the causal relationship between supervision and treatment face considerable difficulties both for design and implementation. Yet such studies are vitally necessary if the impact of one on the other is to be fully understood, and if the conduct of both is to profit from improvement.

How the study affected me

I had no idea when I began this research project that it would effect me in such a deep way. This study has been for me both fulfilling and unnerving.

In describing phenomenology, Patton (2002) notes that one of the implications of this perspective is methodological, "The only way for us to really know what another person experiences is to experience the phenomenon as directly as possible for ourselves" (p. 106). He goes on to quote Van Manen (1990), who asserts, "the essence or nature of an experience has been adequately described in language if the description reawakens or shows us the lived quality and significance of the experience in a fuller and deeper manner" (p. 10).

My experience of conducting this research ranged over many varied and disturbing emotions: anxiety, self-doubt, excitement, frustration, disappointment. It is not lost on me that the feelings I experienced in conducting this study are the same feelings mentioned by most of the people I interviewed. I don't know if it is intrinsically characteristic of phenomenological studies that the researcher ultimately experiences that which the co-researchers are describing, but that seems to have been what happened to me.

This isomorphic process showed up in many ways, through many operations, among many people. It had to do with dialectical processes, co-constructions, mutuality, and other similarly fluid and reinforcing processes. The work of the analysis literally involved moving back and forth, constantly, among parts and wholes of the interview transcripts. I was scanning for connections, checking my assumptions; looking for something missing that I knew was there but had forgotten where.

A similar process accompanied the unfolding of the stories told by the participants. Their stories went back and forth, picking up an important but almost forgotten fragment, moving back and forth in time, struggling for and insisting on the exact expressions to capture accurately the experience. And there was back and forth between the participant and myself, the interviewer. I had questions and needed clarity. The supervisee had a story to tell and needed to be understood. Things moved back and forth, inside and outside. Things came to be known objectively and subjectively. The phenomenological process that I had chosen and, in the beginning, had viewed from afar, objectively, came to have more meaning for me and came to involve me, unwittingly, in the phenomenon. As I said, it was unnerving.

The process took hold and pulled me in. In this, I came to have a deep appreciation of the vulnerabilities that accompany the supervisee—and by extension, the patient—who comes to supervision. Thus, my own empathic capacities were enhanced. I found that I listened to my psychotherapy patients in a new way, with more patience, less judgment. I felt renewed interest in the story my patients were telling and greater courage to invite their reactions and to elicit experiences that lay on the edges of consciousness. I did not shrink from conflict, nor did my patients. I believe I am a better therapist for having done this study.

The methodology was unwieldy at first. It was not apparent to me where the analytic procedures were leading and whether the procedures would, in fact, yield results. As I worked along, my confidence started to expand because I was able to see that something was coming together. Then, as I entered the stage of constructing individual descriptions, I began to recognize the themes and essences emerging through the research process, in answer to the research question. The information that emerged was like gold, the process like sifting for gold. The experience was truly rewarding.

The process took me into the lives of these individuals. Through this method, I moved into the experience of these people, so genuinely that at times I had to stop my work and reside emotionally for a moment with the person whose interview I was analyzing, because I was so affected. I felt that I understood intellectually and emotionally what the person was speaking to. Once having entered into a deep resonance with the person's experience, I felt a responsibility to portray this experience accurately and deeply, to the best of my ability, in order to be true to the person and to her experience. The task expanded beyond the boundaries of pen and paper, keyboard and screen, mind and matter. I felt a responsibility to the individual person of the interviewee.

In relation to all this, I recall a passage from Peter Høeg's novel, *Smilla's Sense of Snow* (1992/1993). I have edited the segment to follow, and despite that adjustment, and the fact that I read the novel in English translation from the Danish, I think the passage relates to some of the things considered here. It provides a literary metaphor for my experience of conducting this study.

Here, Smilla is standing in the doorway, watching as the mechanic prepares dinner. She asks him a question.

"Do you know what the foundation of mathematics is? ... [It] is numbers. If anyone asked me what makes me truly happy, I would say numbers ... . And do you know why?"

He splits the [crab] claws with a nutcracker and pulls out the meat with curved tweezers.

"Because the number system is like human life. First you have the natural numbers. The ones that are whole and positive. The numbers of the small child. But human consciousness expands. The child discovers longing, and do you know what the mathematical expression is for longing?"

He adds cream and some drops of orange juice to the soup.

"The negative numbers. The formalization of the feeling that you are missing something. And human consciousness expands ... and the child discovers the in between spaces. Between stones, between pieces of moss on the stones, between people ...."

(Høag, pp. 112–113)

I like this passage for many reasons. I like the form of the narrative, switching back and forth between Smilla, the speaker, and the mechanic, the one engaged in cooking. I like the tension created by this mechanism of subjective first person alternating with objective description. Both perspectives demonstrate range. Smilla speaks first of numbers, rather cold and hard. But she goes on in her explanation transforming those cold, hard numbers into beautiful, complex human entities. Likewise, the mechanic first cracks open the claw and extracts the meat in a way that's chilling it's so calculating and precise. But then, with almost unbearable sweetness, he flavors the soup with cream and orange juice. I can taste it. There is a counterpoint to the development of this passage, such that each part maintains its integrity, and could stand alone if necessary, but the two parts working together create something new and compelling. I don't think I would be as moved by Smilla's remarks about longing and the in between spaces—and I am moved—if I were not also carrying in my mind the image of the mechanic's efforts to make the soup. The passage is objective and subjective; it is hard and soft, cold and warm. The reader can relate to both. Smilla speaks of filling in the spaces, the in between, between people.

Here there is a meeting of two people, engaged in a conversation and in a project. They bring different qualities and different temperaments to the encounter. They are different; yet they both are vital to the whole. This is what it was like for me to carry out this study.

References

Bacal, H. A. (Ed.). (1998). *Optimal Responsiveness: How Therapists Heal their Patients*. Northvale, NJ: Jason Aronson.

Bernard, J. M., & Goodyear, R. K. (1998). *Fundamentals of Clinical Supervision* (*2nd ed.*). Boston: Allyn & Bacon.

Bruner, J. (1990). *Acts of Meaning*. Cambridge, MA: Harvard University Press.

Creswell, J. W. (1998). *Qualitative Inquiry and Research Design*. Thousand Oaks, CA: Sage.

Ely, M., & Matias, B. D. (2001). A report to the International Institute of Object Relations Therapy. Chevy Chase, MD: IIORT.

Frawley-O'Dea, M. G., & Sarnat, J. E. (2001). *The Supervisory Relationship*. New York: The Guildford Press.

Friedlander, M. L., & Ward, L. G. (1984). Development and validation of the supervisory styles inventory. *Journal of Counseling Psychology, 31*: 541–557.

Høeg, P. (1993). *Smilla's Sense of Snow* (T. Nunnally, Trans.). New York: Farrar, Straus and Giroux.

Husserl, E. (1970). *Logical Investigation*. (J. N. Findlay, Trans.). New York: Humanities Press.

Kaiser, T. L. (1997). *Supervisory Relationships: Exploring the Human Element*. Pacific Grove, CA: Brooks/Cole.

Kindler, A. R. (1998). Optimal responsiveness and psychoanalytic supervision. In H. A. Bacal (Ed.), *Optimal Responsiveness: How Therapists Heal their Patients*. Northvale, NJ: Jason Aronson.

Lincoln, Y. S., & Guba, E. G. (1985). *Naturalistic Inquiry*. Newbury Park, CA: Sage.

Mishler, E. G. (1986). *Research Interviewing*. Cambridge, MA: Harvard University Press.

Moore, B. E., & Fine, B. D. (Eds.). (1990). *Psychoanalytic Terms and Concepts*. New Haven: Yale University Press.

Nelson, M. L., & Friedlander, M. L. (2001). A close look at conflictual supervisory relationships: The trainee's perspective. *Journal of Counseling Psychology, 48*: 384–395.

Olk, M. E., & Friedlander, M. L. (1992). Trainees' experiences of role conflict and role ambiguity in supervisory relationships. *Journal of Counseling Psychology, 39*: 389–397.

Padgett, D. K. (1998). *Qualitative Methods in Social Work Research: Challenges and Rewards*. Thousand Oaks, CA: Sage.

Patton, M. Q. (2002). *Qualitative Research & Evaluation Methods* (3rd ed.). Thousand Oaks, CA: Sage.

Schindelheim, J. (1995). Learning to learn, learning to teach. *Psychoanalytic Inquiry, 15*: 153–168.

Schwandt, T. A. (1997). *Qualitative Inquiry: A Dictionary of Terms*. Thousand Oaks, CA: Sage.

Shanfield, S. B., Matthews, K. L., & Hetherly, V. (1993). What do excellent psychotherapy supervisors do? *American Journal of Psychiatry, 150*: 1081–1084.

Shanfield, S. B., Mohl, P. C., Matthews, K. L., & Hetherly, V. (1992). Quantitative assessment of the behavior of psychotherapy supervisors. *American Journal of Psychiatry, 149*: 352–357.

Stimmel, B. (1995). Resistance to awareness of the supervisor's transference with special reference to the parallel process. *The International Journal of Psychoanalysis, 76*: 609–618.

Van Manen, M. (1990). *Researching Lived experience: Human Science for an Action Sensitive Pedagogy*. New York: State University of New York.

Veach, P. M. (2001). Conflict and counterproductivity in supervision—when relationships are less than ideal: Comment on Nelson and Friedlander (2001) and Gray et al. (2001). *Journal of Counseling Psychology, 48*: 396–400.

Wolf, E. S. (1988). *Treating the Self: Elements of Clinical Self Psychology*. New York: The Guilford Press.

Worthen, V., & McNeill, B. W. (1996). A phenomenological investigation of "good" supervision events. *Journal of Counseling Psychology, 43*: 25–34.

CHAPTER EIGHT

The group supervision model

Colleen Sandor

Supervisors understand that it is difficult to treat traumatized patients. While individual supervision is invaluable in work with traumatized patients, the group supervision model is an often-overlooked modality which may be of particular help. If all goes well, the group provides a safe holding space for the therapist, thereby assisting her in more readily providing a holding space for the patient. During the repeated hostile regressions in which traumatized patients become ensnared, the therapist is frequently the subject of primitive projections, which she must manage and hold. In order to keep the therapy on track, the therapist who is inevitably engaged, and at times lost, in the traumatized patient's internal world is wise to seek supervision. I describe here a way of looking at trauma that I learned in group supervision, and I focus on a particular case to highlight some of the concepts discussed (J. Scharff & D. Scharff, 1994). This group supervision model requires that the therapist learns about her own thoughts, feelings, and behaviors while engaged in the therapy process, so that she can use her full self in the treatment. This is the group affective learning model (J. Scharff & D. Scharff, 2000) applied to group supervision.

Trauma

Object relations theory provides a unique perspective on early trauma and its effects on the internal life of the child and, later, the adult. Early physical and sexual trauma can destroy mental functioning and leave the adult patient with diminished cognitive abilities. Defenses of splitting, repression, and dissociation are engaged in an attempt to restore internal order and mute the noise of the trauma. While these defenses provide solutions for surviving and managing the abuse, the patient is left with an impaired ability to think, a fragmented experience of the internal and external worlds, and therefore tremendous disruption in adult relationships. These cognitive and relational impairments that make daily life difficult become the crux of the therapeutic work as they are played out in the transference and countertransference.

"The analytic literature has not done justice to the complexity of the splits in the self that occur under the impact of trauma" (Scharff & Scharff, 1994, p. 71). In the midst of trauma, the central self splits off the traumatized parts of the self in order to maintain contact with the outside world, and this leaves a rigidly organized internal system of poorly articulated parts of the ego without objects and "of objects divorced from their ego relatedness" (Scharff & Scharff, 1994, p. 73). Consequently, the patient brings a fragmented self to the therapeutic endeavor, the therapeutic space can become split, mirroring the patient's world, and the goal of effective treatment is seriously challenged.

Providing a consistent and safe holding space is critical to the therapeutic work. In fact, one of the main tasks of the therapist is to contain anxiety by taking it in, metabolizing it, and giving it back to the patient in a useable or thinkable form via interpretation (Bion, 1970; J. Scharff & D. Scharff, 1998). Then, the patient feels contained in a number of ways. First, the anxiety has been transformed and is easier to tolerate. Second, the patient feels secure in the knowledge that the therapist has been present to perform this function and has not been destroyed by that which the patient cannot bear. Finally, when the material is given back in the form of an interpretation, the interpretation serves as a linking mechanism, helping the patient make sense of experience, connecting affect with cognition.

Providing containment for a traumatized patient is a challenge for the therapist. In the process of the work, the therapist must allow for confusion and fragmentation to occur, and then help the patient come back together. In this way, the dyad repairs the psychic structure that was either destroyed or co-opted by the traumatic experiences. The therapeutic relationship provides two things that are central to the rebuilding of the patient's psychic structure. The first is that the therapist must provide a safe place for the patient to explore the past trauma—a consistent environment with good boundaries. Scharff and Scharff (1998) call this the contextual holding relationship, to which the patient expresses the contextual transference. The second is to be fully present as an object for projective and introjective identification—the focused relationship, to which the patient develops a focused transference. Once we are projected into, we speak about our experience and make it available for analysis so that our patient may then use the information and develop self understanding. The extent and degree of trauma makes these tasks daunting. Nevertheless both types of transference experiences are required if the patient is to begin to heal.

At times both patient and therapist will feel the terror of the trauma (Hedges, 2000). This can come in the form of a patient's violent regression in which accusations are focused on the therapist, and both are lost in the abyss of negative affect seemingly with no way out. Hedges urges therapists to look into the face of fear, and, holding steady, work it through. This requires us to drop into the mire of the patient's fragmented internal world, thereby providing a space where the splits may be repaired. Hedges cautions us that, if not enough space is given for fragmentation and confusion to occur, the therapy may not progress. If we keep things too neat and tidy, the frightening but necessary patient regressions will not occur. Keeping things in order, the therapist colludes with the patient's defensive structure, thus avoiding any deep affective work. A rigid approach on the part of the therapist parallels the rigidity in the patient's defensive structure.

As therapists, we keep in mind that the therapeutic task is to maintain boundaries and structure a therapeutic frame that allows an adequate holding space for the regression to occur. This is a precarious balance, especially in light of violent regressions and large internal splits of the sort shown in the supervised therapy session to be described here.

Supervision

When we work with patients whose abuse is of tremendous magnitude, we may find it difficult to provide sufficient containment. We may feel overwhelmed by affect, both the patient's and our own. Whether one is a novice or a seasoned clinician treating a difficult case, supervision provides a place to find support, extend knowledge, and develop clinical skill. "Supervision establishes an initial condition within which the development of knowledge can occur" (J. Scharff & D. Scharff, 2000, p. 314). The supervision task is similar to the therapeutic task in a limited way in that good boundaries and a strong frame enable the supervisee to feel safe enough to reveal fully the experience with the patient. The supervisor's perspective and the process of thinking together give the therapist a safe place to examine uncomfortable or puzzling affective reactions to the patient—and to the supervisor. The therapist may project affect evoked in the therapy sessions onto the supervisor in the effort to learn about what is happening. The supervisor functions as a container to help digest what the therapist feels is unbearable. Thus, the therapist and supervisor are engaged in a process that mirrors that of the therapist and patient.

When working with therapists who deal with traumatized patients, a good supervision provides a good holding environment, which in turn helps the therapist provide a similar holding environment for the patient. The trickle-down effect allows the therapist to tolerate the terrifying transference and regressions of the patient, thus making her steady in the work. Scharff and Scharff (2000) write: "As supervisors we maintain a focus on the therapist's view of the patient–therapist relationship. We look at how the patient's psychic structure and unconscious object relations make their impact on the personality of the therapist. We notice how the therapist responds and communicates understanding to the patient on the basis of the appreciation of the transference gained by monitoring and analyzing the countertransference" (p. 315). Good individual supervision may be adequate for a therapist working with tremendous internal splits, regression and dissociation. However, I have found that group supervision provides therapists with a stronger frame, and a broader holding context in which to learn about their fears and tolerate the patient's primitive anxieties. In a group supervision setting, the task of facilitating the learning and containing the affect rests not only on the supervisor but on each group participant, and on the group process. The group functions as an extended holding capacity that is extremely valuable for those therapists who work with trauma.

A safe environment is essential to the supervision process in order for learning to occur. The supervisor facilitates the learning in a safe but confrontational way. The good supervisor has respect for the supervisee and the supervision process, has courage and frankness, shows an open attitude as a learner, is empathic and intuitive, has an attitude of inquiry and reflectiveness, and is open to personal associations (De le Torre & Applebaum, 1974; Scharff, 2005).

In a group supervision setting, each individual member of the group needs to posses these qualities as well. It is critical to the learning process that group members have respect and empathy for one another, show the courage to confront one another, and be frank in their feedback. It is important to remain open as a learner, engage in the reflective process, and become personally and interpersonally inquiring. Supervision group members need to be open to personal associations and have the courage to share these associations. Each member must be adaptable. If any one of these qualities is not present in a single member, its absence can affect that member's learning and participation and change the climate of the group. For instance, a group member who is closed to the process of inquiry and reflection may shut down exploration of her work, and make it feel unsafe for others to share their associations about their own work as well. Over time that sets a tone for the group. The group as a whole is responsible for the contextual and focused transferences recreated in supervision.

Difficulties in a supervision group may be due not only to certain supervisees' characteristics, but also to the material presented. There may be an interaction between the content of the material and the issues of one or another individual member or of the group as a whole. Traumatic material may shut down the group's internal process, rendering the group unable to think, much as trauma shuts down the patient's internal process. Members of the group can mirror various aspects of the patient's self and thus embody the fragmentation. For example, if one group member is particularly shut down this may reflect a withdrawn part of the patient. Or one group member may become overly critical of the material being presented or interpretations being made, thus mirroring the way in which the patient attacks the therapist, in resonance with the way that an internal object is persecutory to the traumatized patient. Eventually, if the group can reveal and come to understand its own internal splits, then the therapist may be helped to hold the promise of integration for the patient, and can then bring this hope back to the next therapy session in the form of stronger containment and greater insight.

The group supervision process that weathers these challenges can be an exceptionally powerful place for learning to occur. Not only is the therapist held by the supervisor but by the group as well. The influence of the group as a community bolsters the therapist in a way that allows her to go back into the therapy with the whole group in mind. The therapist internalizes the group and takes this good internal object into the therapy in the form of a benevolent gang of friends and supporters. The gang helps the therapist face and deal with the terrifying transferences brought out by the traumatized patient.

Affective learning in group supervision

Supervision provides the therapist with a cognitive and theoretical understanding of the work through suggested readings, insights from group members, and the perspective of the seasoned clinical supervisor. However, this perspective may not be enough in the midst of confusing and difficult transference enactments. A deeper and more comprehensive understanding of the therapy can be gained by linking affect with cognition. "What is needed is a model that brings together the therapist's affect and cognition so as to lead to integrated understanding of the patient's experience and the therapeutic relationship" (J. Scharff & D. Scharff, 2000, p. 109).

This model, which incorporates learning at both the cognitive and affective level, can be applied to many areas. One realm is the supervision process. Primitive regressions and difficult transferences cannot simply be held cognitively. They must be internalized by the therapist, processed at both an intellectual and emotional level, and then returned to the patient in a useable form, thus helping the patient change their internal world. Scharff and Scharff (2000) note the importance of teaching therapists this skill: "Traditional training focuses on the intrapsychic dimension of the patient. Traditional supervision encourages the clinician to analyze the transference without involving the self of the analyst, as if the observing, emoting, and mentating functions could be hermetically sealed" (p. 109). Involving the self allows the therapist to have deeper understanding of the transferences and regressions through which to assist the patient in understanding them.

Supervision of a traumatized patient

Madison is a woman in her late 40s who has been a patient for seven years and is currently in twice weekly therapy. She was raised by her mother, and met her biological father only once. From a very early age she was physically, sexually, and verbally abused by her mother until she was 18. Madison's mother used fingers and various objects to stimulate and penetrate Madison's vagina and, when in a particularly crazy mood, she would then cut her genitals. Madison's mother was severely alcoholic and promiscuous. She had men in and out of the home. Most of these men sexually abused and raped Madison. Madison also says that on several occasions her mother tried to kill her. Once her mother filled a bathtub with cold water and held Madison under until she lost consciousness. The abuse continued until Madison left the house at the age of 18.

Madison says her mother used to put her into trance-like states and give her commands over the telephone. She used television to brainwash her, which she accomplished by making her watch violent television shows for hours and depriving her of sleep and food until Madison could no longer differentiate between reality and television. Madison currently does not own a television because, if she begins to watch, she will not "come to" until hours later. As an adult Madison has fallen into particularly regressed and dissociated states. She has many internal splits, some of which in the past came out in the form of other personalities.

Prior to this therapy Madison was in treatment with another therapist for 9 years. During the course of that treatment the therapist had literally tied Madison up, rationalizing that this would enable her to express her anger. During one of these sessions Madison freed herself from the binds and subsequently tied up the therapist, almost strangling her in the process. They continued to work together but, according to Madison, they never spoke of this incident. Madison says she feels like the former therapist told her to get angry, gave her permission to open up her emotions, and then didn't help her learn to do anything with them. She was left feeling very confused and "dropped" by the whole episode.

Context for the sessions

I had been attending a supervision group for some time and the group knew me and my patient Madison quite well. Toward the end of the session prior to the one to be presented here, Madison paid me for the previous month but the amount she paid me was only half of what she owed. Our arrangement was that Madison would pay me $150 for each month of treatment regardless of how many times a week she attended sessions. When I addressed it with her briefly, she said she had "money issues." The current session opens where the last session left off. I usually do not begin the session with a particular topic but I had to address the money issue and what it meant for the continuation of the therapy. During the session, I got stuck in a power struggle over the money, not understanding what it represented. This resulted in a terrifying regression.

The internal supervision group served as my benevolent "internal gang" and held me during this moment. Their support allowed me to recover from a stalemate, stay present, and provide a holding environment for my patient. Then when we met in supervision after the session, their responses helped me to understand that the patient had felt threatened in the therapy process, had regressed, and had a difficult time distinguishing me from her mother. The group's sincere understanding of my experience was reassuring to me at a time of vulnerability and strengthening to my future efforts with the patient.

Session 1: before supervision

THERAPIST: We ended last time with you saying you have some money issues.

MADISON: Aren't there 101 other things that are important for us to talk about?

THERAPIST: We'll get to those. So, about the money issues? You only paid for half of the month.

MADISON: I didn't pay for "only half." I didn't come some of the times.

THERAPIST: Our arrangement was that you pay the fee for the month regardless of how many times you come. That's what we had written up and agreed to and your words about that were, "Oh, so now I can't run away."

MADISON: That doesn't mean I didn't not pay.

THERAPIST: Our arrangement is $150 a month regardless of how often you come.

MADISON: Yeah, but you take off for vacations.

Madison is referring to the week I took off between Christmas and New Year two months earlier. I am feeling frustrated. I see that I am getting into a power struggle with the patient. I find myself wondering what my supervisor will think about this session and whether my colleagues in group would handle it differently or feel just as bound up as I did. At this moment the whole group was in the room with me and I wondered if they would be critical of me.

THERAPIST: Our arrangement is $150 a month and paying me half of that while you are giving money to other people suggests you are angry with me. Paying half of the fee is a way of expressing your anger at me.

MADISON: You are so off. You are mad that I only paid you half. Admit it!

At this point I am beginning to feel inadequate. I feel like whatever I say will be attacked and I am being reduced to half a therapist. I am not able to access it in the session but when I reflect on the work later I realize that Madison is projecting her feelings of inadequacy into me.

THERAPIST: Yes, I am angry you only paid me half. I think the fact that you only paid me half is about your anger here.

My supervisor had said to me recently that I should increase my confrontation with her and that is what I am trying to do. He thought she had reintegrated to a sufficient degree that she could face her own anger and the anger she set off in me without dangerous disintegration. He is in my mind and I am using him differently in this session by staying with the issue in light of the patient's increasing anger. But I find myself still in this power struggle and not knowing how to get out of it. I wonder what my supervisor, and the group, will say about this, now.

MADISON: It's not an attack on the therapy. I paid you so what's the big deal? What's the attack?

THERAPIST: (*Repeating myself, and not knowing how else to say it*). The attack is paying half when we made an arrangement to pay the full amount, and I know you have the money because you are giving money away.

MADISON: So what if I am giving money away to other people? So what? You get paid. Why is it a big deal to you? So I missed it by three days. There's your money, take it! (Sounding very angry, she tosses the check onto the coffee table toward me in a nasty, violent gesture).

THERAPIST: I wonder if we could think about this together, and figure out what it means.

MADISON: What do you think, huh? What do you think?

THERAPIST: I think the anger is getting in the way of our work together.

MADISON: My anger has been getting in the way of something for a long time now. If you think it has just come up recently then well uh … You got paid. Now that I paid you, it's not an attack on therapy. What the hell! It's only one fucking day.

I feel so stuck. We continue for quite some time like this, talking about her anger.

MADISON: Fuck you!

THERAPIST: What is making you so angry about talking about money?

MADISON: I pay you no matter what. Get me a receipt, would ya?

THERAPIST: It's clear in my mind that you pay me but I am talking about the attack on therapy.

MADISON: Then what the hell is the issue?

THERAPIST: Paying only half what's owed is an attack on therapy. This is a critical therapeutic issue.

MADISON: Pissin' you off, am I?

THERAPIST: No.

MADISON: You don't look like I'm not pissin' you off.

THERAPIST: Are you trying to piss me off?

MADISON: I don't need to try. You are already pissed off at me anyway. You are pissed off about the money and pissed off that I am angry with you. You keep making the same statement, and I'm telling you I paid you. What's the big fucking deal? It's only one day late. So there's your money! It's over.

THERAPIST: It's not over. It is still between us. (*I am trying to stay with the confrontation but am not sure if it the right thing to do. Now I see beyond it vaguely, and try something else. The internal group is now feeling insufficient, I am having a hard time accessing it and thinking of how they could be helpful.*) And there is something else between us right now, and I'm not sure what it is.

MADISON: Well if I knew what it was, I would exactly say it. You fucked me over the other day.

THERAPIST: How?

MADISON: You said I was having a traumatic experience in order to make you come back from holiday and I wasn't. I'm not in your fuckin' fan club for fun, and that remark hurt. I didn't have a trauma because you were goin' on a fuckin' holiday. I had to explain that it happened to me a long fuckin' time ago but it doesn't matter. It doesn't matter worth a shit. I don't tell ya just to get fuckin' kudos and make you feel good.

THERAPIST: It made me feel good?

MADISON: You told me that I was having a traumatic experience just to get you back from holiday.

THERAPIST: That's not what I said. (*I feel I have to defend myself and do not feel good about the position I am in. I feel back on my heels, like I am back pedaling.*)

MADISON: You're so damn smart you can walk circles around me, and you're right.

THERAPIST: Do you think that is what I do?

MADISON: Yeah of course it is what you do. That's what everyone else is doing. I never have the correct responses. (*I feel that I don't have the correct responses either.*) You told me I was having a traumatic experience to make you come back from a holiday. (*I feel like the power struggle is continuing and that I have to defend myself*). It stopped me from talking, it shut me down, and it made me feel like I didn't have trust. I'm not in your fucking fan club. I'm not here to give you kudos because you are a better person and I am not. I'm paying for it, and I'm tired of paying.

THERAPIST: I imagine our work makes you feel like you are paying too much for it.

MADISON: I'm tired of paying. What do you want me to do? I'm sick of giving money to you. I don't want to anymore.

THERAPIST: I imagine you are tired of paying for therapy sometimes too. (*What I really mean to say is paying in therapy but since I am feeling so stuck I cannot find the words in the moment*).

MADISON: I'm tired of being me, tired of being generous, tired of being quiet. Tired of sending that check in the mail!

(I see that she has an enraged look. I am not sure what she is talking about but I begin to feel terror in the transference. I know this is a primitive projection and I am wondering if I will have the wherewithal to weather what feels like an in impending fire storm).

THERAPIST: Do you think I need you to be quiet? *(At this point I can see that there has been a shift and I am not sure who I am to her, her mother or her former therapist. I am feeling like I am beginning to scramble on the inside, trying to find my footing. I also feel paralyzed and am trying very hard to stay present in the terror).*

MADISON: I'm tired of you blackmailing me. I'm just tired of it. You tell me to keep my mouth shut. You told me you would go to the cops. I always put your check in the mail. I hate it. I'm tired of calling. I just want to be .... I'm just tired of it. I want you to be dead. I'm tired of sending the check. I'm tired of it, I'm just tired, can't fight you no more, can't not tell. I'm tired of it. I should just kill you.

At this point I am terrified. I don't know if I will be attacked like the former therapist. All I can think of is letting Madison know I hear her in an effort to maintain some sort of connection.

THERAPIST: I hear that you are angry. I hear that you are confused.

MADISON: I'm not confused. I know what I have to do. I'm not confused anymore. I should have done this a long time ago. I hate you! There are no good guys no more. No one knows me. I'm tired.

THERAPIST: Where did the good guys go?

MADISON: They're gone. Sometimes I can't tell the difference between my mom and my former therapist. I'm frightened I'll hurt someone.

THERAPIST: You're frightened you'll hurt me?

MADISON: (Nodding).

THERAPIST: What's happening? (Long pause). You're feeling all upside down aren't you? Turned inside out? *(Here I use my countertransference experience. I was feeling turned inside out and thought she must be feeling that too).*

MADISON: Yeah.

THERAPIST: Are you getting in trouble for telling me what you did? (*At this point I am feeling like I am back on my feet, the moment of terror having passed*).

MADISON: I used to send my mother money.

THERAPIST: You sent her a check every week?

MADISON: Every month.

THERAPIST: For how much?

MADISON: Half of whatever I made. (*Here I am beginning to gain an understanding of how she is treating me like her mother. In the midst of the terrifying transference I become Madison's mother for her*).

At the supervision group

I recall coming to this supervision group eager to share the work and receive direction about it. I had felt lost during much of the therapy session and anxious about what had happened. I felt as if I wanted to expel my feelings of helplessness, inadequacy, and fear into the group, and leave them there. Certainly I wanted my supervisor and fellow supervisees to digest the material for me, and give it back to me in a useable form. I had been working with Madison for so long that at times I underestimated her level of anger and my level of fear. The group helped bring this to the surface. In a group supervision setting, it is not unusual for each member to take on a specific role with regard to the material being presented.

One of the members, who typically is the emotional barometer of the supervision group, helped me see more clearly the level of Madison's affect. During this supervision session, she bristled at the degree of anger Madison was expressing, saying that she was feeling intense fear and concern for me as I recounted the therapy session. This helped me recognize the amount of hostility present and how much I was flooded with fear during the session. It also put me in touch with how stuck I felt in the midst of the power struggle. All of the group members talked about how they would not know what to do in the moment when Madison confused me with her mother. One member described his surprise that I was even able to stay in the room and continue to work in the presence of such rage. He commented that he had trouble thinking, just as I had, which normalized my response. This allowed me to think about the countertransference in regards to Madison rather than getting stuck in a self-critical mode. I was able to see that it was not unusual for me to have been at a loss for words and that I had done well just to keep the focus on the treatment. While I felt lost during most of the session, the critical point was that I was able to hold the space open for the terrifying transference to occur. This, he said, allowed, Madison to regress, fragment, and then come back together and work not only in the current session but in subsequent sessions as well. The group also had many starts and stops in its process which mirrored the flow of the session with Madison that day.

Another member is frequently an intellectual container for the group. She is particularly skilled at breaking down what is happening in the transference and making links between aspects of the material within the session and between it and other sessions and the history of the patient as well. During this session this group member articulated how fragmented the patient was and how this caused me to feel fragmented, which rendered me unable to think. Through the group member's feedback it became clear to me that both Madison and I had lost track of ourselves. In her confusion Madison confused me with her mother and her former therapist, and I felt confused in my thinking. I was also frightened that I might literally be attacked, as the former therapist had been. While the group member acknowledged the affect in the session she also provided cognitive understanding that allowed connection with the affect. The cognitive link helped me see that a parallel process was occurring in the therapy. Madison and I were both unable to think. This group member also linked this session to previous sessions and to Madison's previous treatment where she physically attacked her therapist. For instance, there had been an earlier session where I felt physically threatened by Madison. I raised my voice in response to this threat, and the colleague whose office is next to mine commented that he thought he was going to have to intervene. I have a tendency to minimize the threat of violence but this group member continues to remind me of it and points out how it influences my work with Madison and my level of fear at times.

The supervisor made several helpful comments. First, one of the things he pointed out was that Madison's enactment with money in the session was not as much an attack on the therapy as it was a direct attack on me by way of bringing the issue into the therapy. Having felt her rage in previous sessions, I was more than happy to shift the focus of the attack onto the therapy rather than on me. I think this abstraction was my way of protecting myself from her anger thereby diluting the affect in the moment. He also noted that I was being very active in the session, more active than usual, talking too much. He recommended that I approach the work more quietly. I felt somewhat self-conscious and embarrassed about presenting the material because I was aware that I was overactive. I felt as if I had filled the space too much, and that this resulted in a power struggle.

The supervisor predicted that, in future sessions with Madison, the calmer I became the more Madison would become angry. He said that my remaining calm was crucial because it would allow her to hate me safely and in a constructive way. While I agreed with him I certainly was not looking forward to being hated by Madison, as I knew the potential level of her rage. I felt annoyed at my supervisor because it was easy for him to say this, whereas I would have to be the one to sit through it with her. The group members concurred with me on this point, saying that no one wanted to be in my position. There was a moment of humor in the group that served to break up the intensity of the emotions in the room.

The supervisor suggested an interpretation that I could make to Madison, that at times she must feel like I am torturing her and getting paid for it. He said I should focus on how she feels like she is paying enough just by paying me anything. He also instructed me to address the boundaries with Madison. He grasped the point that at the end of the session Madison showed me how she had made me into her mother. At the point in the session when Madison confuses me with her mother, he suggested I say, "I think you just slipped over a boundary. You went from thinking I am like your mother to thinking I am your mother." The supervisor said I need to demonstrate that I am in favor of everything she is saying as important to the therapy, but that when she collapses I need to pull her back from disintegration. The group had discussed the need for reality checks with patients whose reality testing could slip in the middle of affective storms. I thought this was an excellent suggestion. I found myself wishing I would have been able to think of it in the middle of the session with Madison. I recall feeling terrified and paralyzed at the moment she began to confuse me with her mother. I knew she had been violent with her previous therapist and I wondered if that was what was in store for me.

Finally, the supervisor commented that at the end of the session Madison and I got away from the fact that we had had a confrontation in the beginning of the hour. I know in the session I was glad it didn't come back up. He suggested that a way I can address this is to say that the way she treated me around the discussion of the issue of payment was similar to how her mother treated her, and that working like this helps us understand how painful and frightening that relationship was for Madison. He also pointed out that I could show her that paying me half was a way of bringing this memory of her mother to our own work.

Session 2: a dream following supervision:

In the next session, Madison was able to be mad at me, and our relationship is still in one piece. Madison is slowly coming to understand that I will not be destroyed by her hatred, unlike the way she felt destroyed by her mother's hatred. I felt supported to remain intact and continue to provide a holding environment for her.

The session after supervision, Madison brought in a dream. We were able to work with it and find meaning that related to the previous session. Specifically, we talked about how when something comes "out of the blue" in our work it terrifies her (like the frightening experience of confusing me with the mother she had to pay, or on occasions when there is an insight or a shift in our work). We relate this to how terrifying it must have been for Madison that her mother's violence would often "come out of the blue". We also gained insight into how the enactment with money has a direct tie to how Madison related to money with her mother. Basically she had to pay her mother so her mother would not destroy her.

The dream

MADISON: I am running down an alley and it is dark and wet and raining and black and blue. I open a door and all there is, is space. It is white, and it is so bright I can't see nothing.

THERAPIST: Say more about the space.

MADISON: It's white, it's the therapy space, and the color is red and white. It is very bright and I see it right away. There's a big, whiter space without red.

THERAPIST: What do you think about a big white space without red? (*In contrast to the previous session I am aware of how much more centered I feel, how I am able to work more freely, and I am also quieter, allowing more space for Madison).*

MADISON: I don't see it ever without red. It starts with one drop and it runs down the wall. It's dripping. The only time there is blood on the wall is when I open the door from the alley. You're in the white space and there is no blood.

THERAPIST: What do I represent in the white space?

MADISON: You're pure. In the white space, you're dressed in white, barefoot, and you have a gold chain and gold earrings, your chair is white too, your glasses are off, and you put them on and you stand up, and you're reading a white book. I open the door and make a noise, and you look up. Then you close the book and there is white noise, and then you turn and stand up. You're not expecting me and you were studying about ambition and drive. You're not expecting me.

THERAPIST: The place is pure. What else?

MADISON: It's not as cold as in here (*my office*). It's just right in the white space. The noise is ambition and drive, and I'm not ambitious and I have no drive. The book is knowledge, and there is only knowledge here because you are in the room. A room has no knowledge. A room has memories but it has no knowledge. A room has memories of people in the room. The alley is black and blue, dark and angry, violent. I want to get away and out of the cold. Why are we talking about this? How is it helping me be a better person?

THERAPIST: We are working with the imagery. (*Here I momentarily feel I have to defend myself and the work. I don't like my response but feel caught off guard, like her question came out of the blue. I feel that I'm on the spot and can't think quickly enough*).

MADISON: What are you working on?

THERAPIST: What is it that you are reaching for, that you cannot get to? (*I feel like I recover much more quickly than in the previous session, no doubt due to the supervision I received. The group is with me and is a benevolent presence*).

MADISON: I want to get into the white room because it is safe but I don't want to get it dirty. I get it dirty as soon as I open the door.

THERAPIST: You ruin the white room?

MADISON: My thoughts and memories will ruin the white room because of my past and my present.

THERAPIST: You don't have the idea that the white room can transform you?

MADISON: No I don't have that idea.

THERAPIST: What about the hope that you can gain knowledge and be changed by the white room? (*I am wondering how much of the hope I am holding for her. In the terrifying moments the group holds the hope for the treatment for me. Having given it back to me in the supervision session I want to give it back to Madison so she may feel some hope as well*).

MADISON: There's no hope I would ever be in the white room 'cause I don't believe I am capable of being part of the white room. It's my blood on the wall.

THERAPIST: You feel damaged and the damage is going to keep you from the white room, keep you from getting somewhere you want to go.

MADISON: I feel an immediate reaction to the red on the white. I'm shocked it's my blood that's on the white. It's fresh, immediate.

THERAPIST: Do you feel dizzy right now? (*Again I use my countertransference feelings as I am beginning to feel dizzy*).

MADISON: Yeah! How did you know that?

THERAPIST: Because I feel it too. (*I'm not sure in the moment about making this disclosure but it seems to work out. Madison appears to feel understood by me and is surprised by that understanding*).

MADISON: You do?

THERAPIST: Uhuh. It's like when you run out of the alley and into the room and there is blood—that's what happens when things come out of the blue.

MADISON: (laughing) It's a surprise!

THERAPIST: Any sort of surprise in here terrifies you. You react to any surprise like when there is a shift in our work and it feels like it comes out of the blue.

MADISON: And my reaction is immediate for me.

THERAPIST: Raw.

MADISON: Yeah, raw and fresh and violent.

THERAPIST: When things come out of the blue they are terrifying.

MADISON: More than terrifying.

THERAPIST: Yes and they make you feel violent.

MADISON: Make me feel sick, sad, frightened, dizzy, very scared. It's
            a violent reaction. Change is very hard for me.

At the end of the session I felt better about the work. The holding environment provided to me by the group allowed me to create more space in the room and Madison responded by being able to work with the dream. However, I was left to wonder if I should have made more explicit links to the previous session, and why I hadn't. While with the help of the group I had tolerated Madison's anger, there was a part of me that wanted to forget about it, not incite it again as it is always just below the surface. I also wondered what would come out of the blue next, and how we would both handle it in the future. I knew that we had weathered the storm of this terrifying transference but I also knew that there were others on the horizon, and that I would need the group again to manage them.

The value of group supervision

What was invaluable in the group supervision session was the blending of cognitive and affective understanding. The group internalized the terrifying transference, held it, and then gave it back to me in a digested form, providing me with emotional and intellectual understanding of the session. This helped me work more freely in the therapy.

One of the most useful things about group supervision is that all of the members will provide bits of insight and the supervisor can act as a container by synthesizing them into a whole. For instance, in this supervision session one member held the affect while another held the intellectual understanding. The supervisor was able to take all of the group fragments and pull them together; much like the therapist does for the patient in the session. Both the group members and the supervisor helped me make links in the session material I would not have otherwise been able to make, given how overwhelmed I had felt during the process of the session. I believe that their ability to do this allowed me to go back to the work and provide linking, understanding, and integration for the patient. In the therapy session following this supervision experience, I was able to create more space and experience less fear because of the containment provided by the group. The work with the group helped me feel more certain that I could look in the face of fear and drop into the fragmentation of Madison's world, and so facilitate a repair in the internal splits. I entered the work much more confident in my ability to think and maintain a position of equanimity, regardless of the powerful impact of the affect in the room.

References

Bion, W. R. (1970). *Attention and Interpretation: A Scientific Approach to Insight in Psycho-Analysis and Groups*. London: Tavistock.

De le Torre, J. and Applebaum, A. (1974). Use and misuse of clichés in clinical supervision. *Archives of General Psychiatry, 31*(3): 302–306.

Hedges, L. E. (2000). *Terrifying Transferences: Aftershock of Childhood Trauma*. Northvale, NJ: Jason Aronson.

Scharff, J. & Scharff, D. (1994). *Object Relations Therapy of Physical and Sexual Trauma*. Northvale, NJ: Jason Aronson.

Scharff, J. & Scharff, D. (1998). *Object Relations Individual Therapy*. Northvale, NJ: Jason Aronson.

Scharff, J. & Scharff, D. (2000). *Tuning the Therapeutic Instrument*. Northvale, NJ: Jason Aronson.

Scharff, J. & Scharff, D. (2005). *The Primer of Object Relations. Second Edition*. Lanham, MD: Jason Aronson.

CHAPTER NINE

"Can you hear me?" Cross-cultural supervision by videochat

Christine Norman, Joyce Y. Chen,
Xiaoyan (Katherine) Chen, Chunyan Wu

The use of audio and video communication is making great in-roads in the therapeutic community. Yet it remains controversial. For many therapists, the use of video chat provides significantly more options for enhanced learning and advanced supervision. This is especially true in China where a new generation of therapists is eager to learn about psychotherapy and advance their therapeutic skills, but have limited access to training. Controversy centers on whether it is possible to do quality work that meets a standard equivalent to that of in-person supervision and whether it is possible for a Western supervisor speaking only English to supervise the work of a therapist working in Chinese with Chinese patients. We addressed these issues in a discussion at the final meeting of a supervision group consisting of three Chinese therapists, Joyce Chen, Katherine Chen and Chunyun Wu and an American supervisor, Christine Norman, meeting weekly over the Internet. The supervisees sometimes were in the same room in Shanghai, but more often at home or at work, while the supervisor was in Bolivia. This supervision was arranged through The China America Psychoanalytic Alliance (CAPA). The three Chinese therapists who were living in China, already working in the mental health field, and had established private practices in China, were completing the

CAPA two-year certificate program in psychodynamic psychotherapy in which the supervisor taught and supervised. The supervisor had had previous experience of teaching and learning using audio and video communication at the International Psychotherapy Institute (IPI) when she lived in Salt Lake City, Utah and attended a course in infant observation taught from London by videoconference. She later taught Infant Observation herself from Salt Lake City, using audio conferencing.

The supervision for the Chinese therapists was arranged for a period of 90 minutes on a weekly basis for 32 weeks. Each week, two of the three therapists in rotation presented an on-going therapy for 45 minutes each. Session notes were distributed by email before each session. During the discussion, all group members were encouraged to respond to the material with their own thoughts and associations. In the last meeting of the supervision group, we reviewed the efficacy of the supervision group. Based on that discussion, we will now review cross-cultural barriers to teaching and learning psychotherapy, cultural influences on patients and the conduct of therapy, the effect of supervision on therapy, and the efficacy of clinical supervision conducted over the internet.

The experience of video-chat in supervision

SUPERVISOR: Each of you has been involved in different types of supervision. How do you feel about using video chat for supervision in comparison? What do you think are the strengths and weaknesses?

JOYCE: One of the most attractive aspects of internet supervision is that it allows great flexibility in overcoming time and space limitations. Instead of traveling across the city to see a supervisor, we can meet from home or the office. It saves us time, and many more time slots are possible, even early mornings or late at night. It allows people from different continents and ways of working to meet without incurring the cost of overseas travel. Famous supervisors can be available to many students in different countries. Because of the accessibility and convenience, it makes supervision more affordable, which indirectly improves the quality of mental health care in China. The same benefit can be reproduced in other countries where psychological therapy is not as well established as in the United States.

CHUNYAN: Internet supervision and the instruction it provides, makes the treatment so much better. It makes the treatment not such a lonely job. The content and quality of the discussion are almost the same as a face-to-face discussion, because of the video link. It is effective in understanding both the patient and the therapist in terms of reactions or responses. There are questions, open discussions and progress notes which make the supervision very effective.

KATHERINE: I like video supervision; it is efficient and quite helpful, especially in China, because we cannot easily find a good supervisor to have face-to-face supervision. I enjoyed having three students in the group, so we could share our opinions and talk about the cases together. We did experience problems with the reliability of the Internet, but we found we could improve the quality of the connection by minimizing the windows. Even with technical problems from time to time, our small group supervision was a good experience.

SUPERVISOR: We did have to struggle with the technology occasionally. Because I was living in Bolivia at the time, I didn't always have a lot of band-width in my internet connection. But as Katherine has said, we found that closing the video sometimes helped.

CHUNYAN: The biggest challenge was finding a good time to meet because we were in different time zones. The internet connection was sometimes bad too. When our group meeting took place within work hours, sometimes it was affected by job issues, or if we met at home there could be interruptions by our families.

SUPERVISOR: Yes, that was a challenge too; we had to try several different meeting times to see what worked best. Aside from the technology, there are some other concerns about using video chat. Many therapists are concerned that it is difficult to form an authentic relationship over the internet. I personally feel that having some visual contact is important, even if it cannot be maintained for the entire seminar. My own experience has taught me that a powerful learning experience and an intimate bond can be formed using video chat. Over ten years ago, I participated in one of the first Infant Observation Seminars conducted through video conferencing and then later using Skype, at the International Psychotherapy Institute, based in Washington, D.C. The seminar leader, Jeanne Magagna, a specialist in infant observation, was in London; several participants were in Washington, D.C.; and several more in Salt Lake City, Utah. Over the course of three years, the seminar maintained its integrity, even while we changed technology, lost and added participants, and some of us moved to different cities. This experience convinced me that the use of the internet could provide extraordinary teaching and supervising opportunities.

CHUNYAN: I think the strength of video supervision lies in the continuity it provides. During the academic year when our group met weekly, we could follow the treatment of the patients over a period of time. It also helped us to form a peer support group, since after the online discussion the group members liked to talk together. The group learned to work well in terms of discussion, asking and answering questions, and contemplating the treatment from different points of view. Online supervision and seminars fill a deficit in psychotherapy training programs in China. I learned to be sensitive to the need for confidentiality, which is not so much of a concern for other Chinese therapists in my generation. So access to Western therapists trained in the ethics of clinical practice is another benefit from the online supervision.

JOYCE: I agree with many American teachers that the internet itself raises concerns about confidentiality in addition to the frustration of poor transmission quality. However, for Chinese students, having internet supervision is much better than NO SUPERVISION. I have attended trainings offered by German, Canadian, or American teachers who come to China and offer 5 to 7 days of intensive training, and then we are left alone to digest the material. It is hard to integrate all the ideas without the help of an experienced supervisor. Currently, there is very little ongoing supervision offered after training in China, especially in couple therapy. Yet 50% of patients in commercial counseling centers are seeking marital help. If all the training programs could provide internet supervision as an optional follow-up program, I believe it would help new Chinese therapists to grow more steadily.

The effect of cross-cultural supervision

SUPERVISOR: How do you think our different cultural backgrounds affected the supervision? How well do you think we understood each other and did we have any problems with language or understanding cultural norms?

KATHERINE: The ease of communicating and understanding one another was directly related to our level of proficiency in spoken English. It was helpful to talk among ourselves in Chinese if we found something we could not understand in English, and so find a way to communicate with the supervisor. But I believe that at a profound level many aspects of the human condition are universal. For me, our discussions helped me understand my patient's loneliness and fear, not because she was Chinese, but because she was human. For example, my patient, Miss M, felt her mother ignored her and her father devalued her. When she came to see me, she had lived alone for many years and did not have any close relationships. She is a talented business woman, very beautiful and seemed emotionally stable and rational. She gave the impression to friends and to me that she was independent, strong, could handle everything on her own. But in the deepest place of her heart, she was so lonely and had so many fears. She was afraid to have a relationship and found it so difficult to trust people, even those who liked her. In our relationship, I felt it was so difficult to get close to her. She repeatedly complained that therapy was not helping. She had huge anger toward me for a very long time. She was like an angry baby who kept crying all the time, no matter what the mother did for her. Through the supervision, I received so much support and it helped me to understand the unconscious primitive anger this patient had, which is universal, and it did help me to hold this patient well.

JOYCE: Supervision between an American supervisor and Chinese students does require the Chinese supervisees to have good English. They need to be able to write their session notes in English, understand the American teacher and carry on a meaningful conversation. The group setting is a good mechanism to help resolve language issues. The students can help one another to translate difficult terms from Chinese to English and vice versa. I remember one example. Therapist A's process notes read: "She'd rather be single, she don't want to be like her parents, having a marriage like a mass." The supervisor asked Therapist A, what did she mean, "having a marriage like a mass?" Therapist A explained her intent to the other supervisees in Chinese, and then together they explained to the supervisor that she had meant to say, "a mess", not "a mass". With group efforts, we could surmount any language barriers in our supervision.

Our supervisor could help us understand some American colloquialisms. Working in English, patient C said, "My mom is funny. She always blows up in conversations and I think she exaggerates a lot." The supervisor told us that the patient meant that her mother was "different or strange", not as we thought, "laughable or ridiculous." Patient C also used the phrase, "I feel ticked" many times. We were not familiar with this expression and the supervisor gave us examples and compared it to frustration and anger. Basically, there are those "read between the lines" statements where we can help one another.

CHUNYAN: It seems Chinese therapists are more familiar with Western values and ideology since we have access to Western cultures through modern media such as Google. com, Youku (YouTube), Facebook, movies, and television series.

SUPERVISOR: I agree that the Chinese students and therapists that I have known have much more knowledge about Western culture, than Westerners have about modern Chinese culture. There are still many stereotypes about the repressive nature of the current Chinese society. When I came to teach English in China in 2009, I was very surprised to find that my students had a wide ranging interest in American culture and knew much more about American history than I knew about Chinese history. I had students who could quote me Martin Luther King's entire speech, "I have a dream. ..." I, on the other hand, could quote only one aphorism, Deng Xiaoping's reference to socialist versus a free market economy: "No matter if it is a white cat or a black cat; as long as it can catch mice, it is a good cat." It amazed me that my students knew so much about America, but I still smile when I remember that their favorite television show was *Desperate Housewives*. I'm not sure that is entirely representative of American culture in general. But using media is a good starting point to try and understand a different culture.

CHUNYAN: When there was a topic related to a cultural issue, the group members asked one another questions and got clarifications, so that the supervision could proceed. We could explain to the American supervisor the reality of the patient's life in Chinese society and the structure of the Chinese family. One example is the one-child policy in China. One of the core values of Confucianism is filial piety, and this still dominates modern Chinese culture. The only child of a family feels under pressure to fulfill the parents' wishes by being successful in their career and marrying to perpetuate the family. Psychological separation from parents is quite difficult for the younger generation. Parents want to keep their children in arms for ever. They organize their child's life by arranging study in university for them and finding them job positions after graduation. The younger generation struggles to meet the expectations and pressure from parents and grandparents, although they get lots of support and concern from them. When the child grows up and wants to move to another city to work, he or she suffers guilty feelings for not being able to live with and take care of their parents, or they take their parents to live with them in the same apartment, so that they can all help one another. This is an example of the current family structure.

SUPERVISOR: I do think that the intense sense of obligation that children feel to please their parents is something I didn't understand until I lived in China. As Chunyan expressed, it is very difficult for most children, even adult children, to refuse their parents or disappoint them. Someone once described it to me as "silken cords of obligation." By this she meant that when the parent has done absolutely everything for the child and has made enormous sacrifices for the child's education and opportunities, the child accepts that they must try to please the parent and sacrifice their own wishes.

CHUNYAN: Obligation is quite a big phenomenon in Chinese culture and society. Most parents take for granted the child's sense of obligation because it is a central value in our long national history. It is seen as an essential part of family harmony and societal harmony. The positive aspect is that it leads to fewer conflicts and supports the child's survival. The parents' wishes are paramount, so it soothes the parents. On the other side, it comes at the expense of the child's individuality. The child can't grow up to be a mature man or woman, partly because the parents do not allow them to be themselves. It causes personality problems or disorders and more separation anxiety problems compared to western cultures. The child will feel guilty or inadequate to have his or her own life.

SUPERVISOR: We often thought about the split in how your patients appeared to others, but how their internal world was very different. For these patients the need to fulfill the wishes and obligations of their parents created a false self.

CHUNYAN: Chinese history for centuries has been centered around an agrarian society. Family harmony has been a fundamental principle that has been worshiped from generation to generation. To respect parents and be obedient to them has been a core value for children to learn and act upon. The current Chinese definition of success is to be an intellectual, to marry and have children. This pressure transfers to our patients. For example, patient B does not want to hurt others or his parents since he can understand their expectations and wishes and thinks they are not unreasonable. He knows it will be a great sorrow if he does not marry and is not professionally successful.

KATHERINE: Of course, the history of a country and more importantly, a family, is a big issue in therapy. As in any culture, Chinese history has affected the Chinese family in complicated ways. So understanding the influence of history on the family helps us to understand the patient better. There is a lot of trauma caused by the history of our country, like the Culture Revolution and the two decades of civil war. My patients, from ages 30 to 50 years old, often have very unhealthy parents, because of intergenerational trauma. It is very complicated and sensitive, but it exists in almost every family. For example, the parents of my patients lived their life with no choice about where they could live, what kind of work they would do, even who they could marry because of some political movements in Chinese history. They do not understand why their children should have the freedom to choose something in their life. And their children, my patients, can identify with their parents' sorrow and so they develop a "false self" to complete the unfulfilled wishes of their parents' and to maintain a strong connection with their family.

Cross-cultural influences on patients

SUPERVISOR: One of the interesting aspects of our supervision group was that it was helpful to think about how Chinese and American cultures were influencing Chinese patients. One patient had been raised by Chinese immigrant parents in the United States, another patient had studied and worked in the United States for a number of years, and another patient had worked extensively in various other countries. It was often helpful to look at some of the therapeutic issues from different cultural perspectives.

JOYCE: Here is an example about the benefit of cross-cultural supervision. My patient could not say NO to her roommate and friend. The roommate insisted that she eat certain things, accompany her when it was inconvenient and do many other things that my patient resented. As a traditional Chinese woman therapist, I felt that the way her friend treated her was "not fair or not nice". When my supervisor used stronger words like, "she is a controlling freak!" it gave me the courage to tell my patient that she should not be treated that way. This in turn empowered my patient to be open to say more about her dissatisfaction with her friend and other aspects of her life.

Another area where I grew as a therapist was my ability to talk about sex or sexual terms such as masturbation or penis in English in supervision, and then in therapy. That's a new experience for me. I have overcome the embarrassment of talking about sexual organs and behaviors.

KATHERINE: It was helpful for me to discuss sex in supervision. Then I could talk about it with my classmates. Then I began to talk about it with my patients in a natural way. I think it is a process. The more we discussed it in a professional way, the better we could discuss it in our practice.

SUPERVISOR: We also had some important discussions about the way Chinese and American culture reacts to homosexuality.

KATHERINE: I think it is more difficult for a homosexual to be accepted in Chinese culture than in American culture.

CHUNYAN: I can give an example. Some Chinese parents have high expectations, but cannot or will not help the child. They expect the child to learn by himself without asking questions. As a child, patient B had this kind of pressure, but with little parental support. He repressed his anger and became quiet at home and in school. He never asked for anything from them. He did not get any support or strength to explore the world and could not even enjoy his time alone. But as a child he still knew his parents' wishes, such as going to a university and being employed—and, of course, being married with a child. The greatest anxiety comes from the pressure to marry, since in China, marriage traditionally stands for being grown-up and the beginning of a real life journey. But what if the patient is gay? For my patient B, it was inconceivable that he could tell his family about his homosexuality. For him, and for most people in China, being homosexual can only be a secret, even though the fact of homosexuality and various sexual behaviors is more open than before. For instance, there are virtual forums online for people to make friends and communicate their anxieties and concerns. However, there are almost no homosexual communities in the real world, because most people do not dare to announce that they are homosexual, since there is still deep discrimination against it. Once people understand that homosexuality is not a psychosis, and that there are biological reasons for it, then they can accept it and take it as a personal choice. Only then can people respect the courage to come out as homosexual and work for gay rights.

The effect of supervision on therapy

SUPERVISOR: I think the most effective part of any group supervision is to access the countertransference of different members of the group. When we could each begin to think about our reactions to the case material or to the process notes we often discovered aspects of the patients' unconscious.

JOYCE: I liked that the supervisor asked the other two members of the group to share their associations and thoughts about the material before offering her opinion. This allowed for different ideas to surface and even to discover some of the unconscious themes that were present, but not talked about openly. Because I got input from three different people on my case, I could see my patient from different perspectives and think about areas I had neglected. Our discussions gave me confidence and direction for the coming sessions.

Through supervision, my Chinese colleagues and my American supervisor helped me see my patient from different perspectives. Her issues are more complicated than

I had thought at the beginning, and she is not as strong as I thought her to be. In supervision, I realized that I was not connecting what she told me; everything was in bits and pieces that just didn't come together to form a clear picture. I learned to use this feeling as part of the countertransference and understand that this was probably how the patient felt about her identity—confused and not integrated. Many parts of this patient are like broken pieces that need to be supported and understood so that they can be thought about.

CHUNYAN: This was also an important part of the supervision for me. I remember one session when I was asked to speak about how I was feeling at the moment. I realized that I felt so empty and discouraged. Then one of the group said that she felt so bored by my patient, almost like he didn't exist. In that moment I began to understand my patient at a deeper level and I could think about his deep despair.

KATHERINE: I had the similar experience of seeing my patient as a strong and independent woman, but as the group reacted to her behavior, I could begin to see the frightened child. In my case, the patient had a very strong negative transference and was verbally demeaning to me and dismissive of the effectiveness of the therapy. I had never had such a negative experience in therapy before. No matter how hard I worked or what progress was made, the patient only saw the negative. It was very difficult to hold on to my belief in the value of therapy, and I began to lose my confidence to work with this patient. But with the strong support of my two classmates and the American supervisor, I felt encouraged and gained the strength to work with this patient. The supervisor explained to me about the primitive aggression a patient could have, and confirmed that what I was doing in the therapy was correct. My classmates continued the encouragement in the week between meetings of the supervision group.

The effectiveness of internet supervision

JOYCE: I liked the design that we could present 2 cases each week, and we had to write process notes. This gave us a very solid session each time. We could learn not only how to work with our own patient, but we also learned from discussing our colleagues' cases.

KATHERINE: I also learned a lot from the other two cases that were presented. Each of my classmates has her own style in therapy, which is different from mine, and that often gave me a new perspective on how to understand the patient. The supervisor was sensitive and experienced, and she encouraged all of us.

JOYCE: One of the major differences between Chinese supervisors and American supervisors is that the Chinese supervisors are much more critical. The Chinese teaching philosophy is that criticism helps a student learn something. One of my colleagues was reduced to tears by her supervisor's criticism. For me, the internet supervision gives me access to a more experienced and warmer supervisor. This not only helps me with my technique in therapy, but also serves as a role model for my own teaching and supervising.

CHUNYAN: Group supervision helped me build a support group not only online, but offline too. Our discussions built an atmosphere of trust between us and we experienced a sense of support that went beyond treating our supervised cases. I feel warm and supported when we talk or I meet them in person. A good relation among colleagues is essential. They provide an emotional safety net, back-up, a referral network, and cooperation for career development. So, online supervision is good for the profession.

Summary

We have explored the strengths and deficits of using video chat to understand therapeutic process, and have considered the challenges of arriving at cross-cultural understanding. As new technologies emerge, often with instant acceptance, we find that we live in a world where we can affect and influence each other in ways we never imagined before. And we find that we have much in common and much to share. The new tool of video-chat allows us to express and extend our desire to understand the human condition, share our knowledge and clinical skill, and support our colleagues to enhance the power of therapeutic process.

The poet Kwame Dawes (2010) gives an elegant way of expressing what we do:

> *learn the healing of talk, the calming*
> *of quarrel, the music of contention,*
> *and in this cacophonic chorus,*
> *we find the ritual of living.*

Reference

Dawes, K. (2010). Talk: for August Wilson. Online at http://www.poets. org/viewmedia.php/prmMID/22007. Accessed December 2, 2012.

CHAPTER TEN

Supervision of the therapist's resonance with her patient

David E. Scharff

In the process of supervision of psychotherapy, we are interested in many aspects of the work from the details of technique to transference and countertransference. One of the richest areas of growth for a trainee at every stage is in the interplay between the professional's personal issues and the issues of the client. In the object relations approach to therapy, we focus our work in this area because this is where we can understand clients from inside their resonance with our own object relations. Similarly, in doing supervision, we focus on the correspondence between the trainee's issues and those of his or her client because here we find the greatest potential for making strengths and vulnerabilities of a therapist fully available for the work of therapy.

The following vignette from supervision offers an opportunity to look at an instance of this interplay that resonated between patients and therapist as it did between therapist and supervisor.

Mrs Mills and the Smith family

Mrs Mills was a moderately experienced therapist of children and adults, who, however, had not been working professionally for the preceding five years while having children. She was reentering the field by taking a training program in object relations family therapy.

I supervised Mrs Mills in the treatment of Mary Smith, a woman in her early twenties, and her family. Mrs Mills met with the family regularly and saw individual members occasionally. Some years before, Mrs Mills, then recently licensed, had seen Mary when she was a homeless adolescent, ejected by her parents for oppositional behavior. Mary kept in touch with Mrs Mills on and off over the next few years. At the time of the supervision, Mary had been in a tumultuous marriage for the previous four years. Her husband, Mr Smith, had an 11-year-old daughter from an earlier marriage. The Smiths now had a 3-year-old boy. But the tragedy in the Smith family centered around the death of their infant daughter less than a year before these sessions. The baby developed a rapidly malignant and horribly deforming tumor at 2 months of age and died at home at 5 months of age. The already borderline Smith family had been coming apart at the seams ever since. Mr and Mrs Smith railed at each other, the 11-year-old girl was angry, and the 3-year-old boy talked incessantly and dominated the family. He was, however, the only one to talk directly about the baby's illness and death.

Mrs Mills was often anxious about this family, who could not discuss the death. They became more chaotic with each reminder. She often wished they would go away, although she felt responsible to help. At the time of the following vignette, the anger between husband and wife had reached a boiling point, and Mr Smith's anger seemed particularly threatening to Mrs Mills. When Mrs Mills thought the husband might be violent, she presented the case to classmates in the family training program's group supervision in such a manner that they were all convinced that he was likely to go out of control and hurt not his wife but Mrs Mills. With their encouragement, Mrs Mills arranged to move an individual session she had scheduled with Mr Smith from her regular office to an office in the suite of a male classmate while he was also seeing patients, so that she would feel protected. In our supervisory session, I could not find anything in the material or history to justify a realistic fear, so I tried to understand her fear as countertransference—although I supported her need to protect herself meanwhile. It was clear that the therapist's fears for her own survival were impairing her capacity to provide containment for this chaotic family, and that these fears were especially prominent in this phase.

The chaos continued. Mary Smith began feeling suicidal as she had before, and on one occasion she stormed out of the house with the 3-year-old boy. A couple of days later, after both a family and a couple session, Mary came back. The couple session had allowed Mr Smith to explore and express his rage that his wife "dumped everything on him." It began to look as though the therapist's fear for her own life when meeting with the husband represented an overidentification with the wife. Mrs Smith's contention that the husband would do something violent to her was, I thought, a projection of her own rage, which Mrs Mills, in her own identification with Mrs Smith, could not see. I asked Mrs Mills if anything occurred to her about her own vulnerability in trying to contain this chaos, the projected rage, and the family's difficulty in mourning the baby's death.

Mrs Mills told me that at age 17, on one day's notice, she had emergency surgery for a mass in her chest. She was convinced she was going to die. Her normally reserved father sat outside the operating room crying. Both parents stayed with her at the hospital. The mass was not malignant, but, as the surgeons could not remove all of it, they contemplated another operation. She vividly recalled being wheeled into a room "full of a hundred doctors" for a case conference.

We agreed that she was identified with the threat to life that this family could not metabolize. When Mrs Mills first met her, Mary Smith had been 16 and abandoned by her parents. The girl's age and her sense of aloneness when her parents were crippled with fear resonated with Mrs Mills' own anxieties during her adolescent surgical threat.

By the next week's supervision, Mrs Mills had reflected more on her surgery and her identification with the wife. She realized that her own parents had been under enormous stress at the time of the surgery, leading to fears for their survival as a couple. During the week, Mrs Mills had a dream:

"In the dream, I am going to face my own surgery, but it is happening now. I said to the doctors, 'I won't let you operate until I write letters to my children.' I wrote letters to each of them, including my baby, telling them how special they are and recalling special moments I've had with them."

Mrs Mills had commented before how hard it was for her to work with this family, because she so often thought of her own healthy young children and because this family made her think about things she would like to forget. Now she remembered being at the funeral of the Smiths' infant. The family was not then in treatment with Mrs Mills, but Mary had been in touch with her during the baby's illness. Looking at the coffin, Mrs Mills had had the fantasy that she could see the baby inside and could see the horrible distortion of the baby's face from the tumor. She had been overwhelmed with sorrow, whose depth had seemed to extend personally even beyond that of the Smiths' tragic situation.

I said that we had both seen that she was identified with Mrs Smith as a frightened adolescent and as the parent of young children. She was also identified with her own mother seen in Mrs Smith as the mother of a dead baby. I said, "You came close to death from a mass yourself as an adolescent."

Mrs Mills wiped a few tears from the corners of her eyes.

After a few moments, I said, "I think this dream means you identify yourself with the dead baby. Maybe you couldn't face that earlier."

She said, "I don't think I ever understood how frightened I was of dying. I was just so mad at my parents for being depressed themselves that I felt like they abandoned me in the hospital. I couldn't understand their fear I would die." Then she sobbed for some minutes.

Recovering, Mrs Mills then pursued the theme of abandonment, the feeling that had consciously dominated her own adolescent experience of surgery. She said that Mary Smith's mother had left when Mary was 4, leaving seven children. Mrs Smith had felt terribly abandoned throughout her life, reenacting it in her adolescence by getting herself ejected by her father and stepmother. We could see that the baby girl who died had represented the patient's fantasied chance to give her daughter the love and care she herself had missed. Because it was Mary's first daughter, the baby had been more of a focus for these hopes than her son. Through the relationship with the baby girl, the patient had hoped to make up for what she never got from or gave to her mother.

I said that things seemed a bit more complex than we had understood. Mrs Mills was identified with Mary, who was herself identified with the dead baby and who was also guiltily reacting to its death as though Mary herself were the abandoning mother she had when she was 16.

Mrs Mills agreed and thought this might explain Mary's becoming suicidal after the death of the infant and again at its first anniversary. We could now trace the effects of this ambivalent identification of the patient with her abandoning mother. The baby's death must have reactivated this desperate bind for her.

We could also see how the whole constellation resonated with Mrs Mills' history. Just as the two living Smith children were not getting what they needed from their depressed parents, and just as the fragile bond of the parental couple was riven by the infant's death, so Mrs Mills had been unable to provide effective holding to the Smith family because of being unable to bear the idea of herself as a dead object and because of her identification with the mother through which she had joined them in their predicament. The Smith family had also become a dying baby to her, and here she became the parent who could not stand the loss and failure.

The identification that we fashioned together in supervision could now provide the means to understand the Smith family, and particularly Mary's dilemma. It enabled Mrs Mills to move toward providing the holding that the family had been unable to provide for itself.

The role of the therapist's unique history

Mrs Mills then asked a question of great interest to us. "But what if I hadn't had my own surgery? How would I know what had happened?"

The answer is that we each have our own unique history, our own internal objects that will resonate with our patients' situations in unique ways to provide us with the clues we need. The issue is not whether a therapist has had surgery or her own acute threat of death. It is that the specific facts of Mrs Mills' personal situation provided her own way of joining with this family and of working with me. Her dream provided us with clues to the countertransference, clues that were consistent with other clues we could now understand.

For instance, Mrs Mills had not wanted to think about her own vulnerability or past situation. At the same time, she had been feeling more and more dread about treating this family. In the supervision sessions, I had been trying to contain her hopelessness about the family's chaos. When I urged Mrs Mills to stick with this family, I felt as though I was brutalizing her. I suffered increasing doubt about my faith in the therapy and in my ability to help Mrs Mills through supervision. I agonized about whether I was exposing her to harm in questioning her judgment about the potential for violence by the husband.

Her experience of feeling threat to her personal survival while trying to help this family was triggered both by her own prior life experience and by factors particular to Mary and the Smith family. The confluence of these produced a crisis in the therapy and in the therapist's training. Mrs Mills began to doubt that she could remain an effective mother to her own children while reentering the field of psychotherapy. Here was a resonance with the Smith family's fears for survival. Mrs Mills doubted that she could care for her own needs and those of her children, and she thought that she might therefore have to let her professional self remain dead.

The therapist's dream was primarily an expression of her personal struggle, which she experienced as she was torn both by the family and by me in the supervision. My urging her on with this family felt to her as though I were the doctor of her own adolescence, pressing dangerous surgery upon her, surgery that threatened her existence now. When she wanted to write to her children before proceeding with the operation, she was telling me, in the supervisory transference, how endangered she felt with my prescription for her work, how our work and her work had threatened to take her away from her children. I was giving her a prescription she felt to resonate with the life-threatening surgery many years before.

For a long time I had felt, in the supervisory countertransference, how threatened Mrs Mills was. I was threatened, too. I acknowledged my own fears for risk and my doubts concerning my supervision. The work on this dream let us both understand from various levels of countertransference how her own fears as a student resonated with the family's internal risk. It allowed us to understand the resonance of the internal experience of risk in the patients, in the therapist, and in me as the supervisor. It was not my task to engage in sustained, in depth analysis of the effects of Mrs Mills' history and unconscious dynamics on her personal life as I would do in analysis or therapy, but this limited exploration gave Mrs Mills new comfort in staying with this family and in her reentry into the field of analytic psychotherapy. And, as her supervisor, I also felt better for having worked this through.

There are threats to personal survival when any of us undertakes a new venture. Some kinds of work, however, accentuate the sense of risk dramatically. Just as a doctor reacts to the threat of the inherent risk in the gravely ill patient by an unconscious accentuation in concern for his or her personal survival, so the psychotherapist learning to deal with high risk patients must react in resonance with his or her personal vulnerability and inevitably will act self-protectively. In a similar way, parents view themselves in new ways and experience threats to their self-esteem as they see the progress and travails of their children. Personal histories of vulnerability are triggered. Those psychotherapy trainees who are the most at risk personally will be most apt to suffer crises of larger proportions. The amount of vulnerability is determined by a blend of personal vulnerability of the therapist and the extent of external stress imposed by the patient or client population.

Therapists all seek to have their identity confirmed by healing their patients. So the interaction of the therapist's object relations with the unconscious of the patient reflects this fundamental hope to repair the object and to help our dependent objects grow as an expression of our own hopes for growth and survival. It is only when the object is made "good-enough" that we can dispel our own fears of damage caused by our envy, greed, anger, and narcissism. The failure of repair of psychotherapy patients, like the death of the medical patient or the faltering of a child, threatens therapists with the evidence of their own destructiveness. This defeat of our efforts at repair also deprives us of an image of a person who can confirm our goodness in return. There is no object to help keep at bay the ever-present possibility of the return of our infantile destructiveness or helplessness against the forces of disintegration.

Vulnerability and learning

A psychotherapy trainee, like a medical trainee, feels his or her own survival is linked to the life-or-death issues of the patient. This situation of vulnerability is also a time of great learning potential. As supervisors and teachers of psychotherapists, we have many chances to work directly to strengthen the vulnerabilities of our students. At times we do so by teaching technical skills or examining transference. At other times, we can facilitate the examination of the relevance of the therapist's personal history to the patient or family's therapeutic situation, as I was able to do in this instance with Mrs Mills. And at all times, we are a model for our trainee-therapists as they take in our ways of working with the unknown, with anxiety, and with the supervisory relationship.

There are complex issues of countertransference for the supervisor. I worried that I might be jeopardizing the safety of my trainee. Was I propelling her into a dangerous or hopeless situation? Yet, I also worried that unless she could develop an understanding that would let her continue with the family, I might not be able to teach her anything worth knowing. My countertransference conflict concerned the question of her safety balanced against her growth. As I struggled, I suffered my own pangs of hopelessness about her and about myself.

We all live with this situation when we supervise psychotherapists who encounter patients at risk. When we support them to confront their internal risk, and especially when we do so by confronting our own sense of being at risk, we offer an opportunity in which it is often possible to transform old vulnerabilities into new strengths-both for our trainees and for ourselves.

CHAPTER ELEVEN

Supervision in the learning matrix

Jill Savege Scharff

It is often assumed that the good therapist will also be a good supervisor. A newly assigned supervisor might receive supervision as a safety check on competence, but that is not always required. Once their appointments are made, supervisors often do not have their supervision work supervised. Regrettably they function autonomously in an area that is unscrutinized, almost as separate from seminars as therapy should be. This means that supervision, an important educational activity, is relatively unexamined. Although some supervisors and their supervisees have welcomed the opportunity to present supervision processes for study at international psychoanalytic meetings, most have not. Ignorance of the meager literature and the assumption that skill as a clinician automatically transfers to teaching clinical skill combine to limit supervision to the unexamined arena of the supervisor-supervisee dyad. These factors restrict the effectiveness of supervision, rob supervisors of support groups, and compromise the development of a comprehensive theory of supervision.

In many institutions, supervisors also evaluate competence with a view to deciding the supervisee's future. This can make supervisees secretive or duplicitous in order to avoid criticism or delay in progression. It can destroy individuality, spontaneity, and creativity if students suppress their independent thoughts in the name of getting through the program. In our view, the student is more free to learn if the supervisor is not required to certify competence against a standard. We agree that the supervisor must evaluate and intervene, but without the burden of having a judgmental or gatekeeping function.

The learning matrix model

We propose a model that provides supervisors with a matrix in which to study supervision. In this model, supervisors relate the supervisory process to the social unconscious and the professional culture in which the treatment is taking place and connect it to the supervisee's learning in the total institution. Gains from the supervision experience are then fed back into the matrix.

What do we mean by supervision? Individual and group supervision are learning settings in which supervisors and supervisees focus on the clinical case and the dynamics of the therapist-patient relationship. Supervision establishes an initial condition within which the development of knowledge can occur.

As chaos theory shows, the organism's sensitivity to initial conditions is acute (Gleick, 1987; D. Scharff, 1998, 2000; J. Scharff & D. Scharff, 1998a). The organism develops a pattern that is shaped by its proximity to a more organized system. The organism in turn influences and is influenced by other patterns of relatedness in neighboring systems that are then said to exert a *strange attractor* effect. The patient–therapist relationship brought to a supervision setting comes in contact with the powerful organizing system of the supervisor's greater experience and superior knowledge that operates like a strange attractor. The dynamic system of the supervisee–supervisor relationship reflects the patient-therapist system and at the same time shapes and guides the supervisee's development and its impact on the patient–therapist relationship.

Supervisors have described a *parallel process* in which issues in the therapeutic relationship are reenacted between the therapist and the supervisor (Arlow, 1963; Searles, 1965b). We prefer to conceptualize the parallel processes found in supervision in terms of chaos theory. We see parallel process as a *fractal*, a similar pattern created in a different level of scale, a dynamic footprint of the therapeutic interaction being described. By its self-similarity to the image of the therapeutic system, the fractal image created in supervision provides a clue to the nature of the therapeutic relationship and the form of the transference and countertransference in the treatment that is being studied. The chaos theory concepts of fractals and strange attractors help us conceptualize how individual patterns of thinking, feeling, and behaving (shown in treatment) interact with others (shown in supervision) and reverberate in systems of mutual influence.

Supervisors oversee the progress of the case and help supervisees extend the range of their clinical understanding and skill. If they discover that the range is limited by a lack of knowledge of theory, they may suggest remedial reading or courses of study, but they do not focus on teaching theory. Supervisors are responsible primarily for providing supervisees with an opportunity to learn technique with a view to developing their therapeutic efficacy. This requires that they think that their work as therapists is good enough to be helpful to the patient, but not optimally so, and that they feel safe enough in the presence of their supervisors to acknowledge those areas of expertise that need to be developed. Supervisors assess these weaknesses of the therapists and find ways of addressing them.

As supervisors, we are there as guides, helpers, supporters, and mentors. Admittedly, we are also there as delegates from the faculty of the institution, and we do need to evaluate the supervisee's learning progress in relation to institutional goals. We must identify dumb, weak, and blind spots for further discussion or analysis (Gross-Doehrman, 1976; Szecsödy, 1994; Wallerstein, 1981). This duality in responsibility sometimes leads to ambiguity and conflict, both of them made worse when supervision evaluations are kept secret and when the institution has a certifying task. We do, however, value the idea of making evaluations, but only if they are standardized and mutual: Evaluations follow a known checklist, they are filled out both by supervisor and supervisee, and the results are openly discussed.

An additional balancing mechanism is provided to counteract dumb, blind, or weak spots in the supervisory function. The supervision experience is open to discussion in faculty meetings. Other faculty members who know of the student's learning style in small- and large-group settings or who have already supervised the student may help the supervisor design interventions to improve the student's application of concepts to the clinical situation.

As supervisors, we maintain a focus on the therapist's view of the patient–therapist relationship. We look at how the patient's psychic structure and unconscious object relations make their impact on the personality of the therapist. We notice how the therapist responds and communicates understanding to the patient on the basis of the appreciation of the transference gained by monitoring and analyzing the countertransference.

Just as the affective learning group may veer toward the therapeutic, the supervision process may by filled with inappropriate affect and unconscious fantasies that are difficult to manage. All the behaviors that arise in the group in response to anxiety about the concepts may be brought into the supervision as well. The supervisee may identify with the patient's unanalyzed aspects and act them out in relation to the supervisor in a parallel process of fractal similarity (Arlow, 1963; J. Scharff & D. Scharff, 1998a; Searles, 1965b) or may aggressively identify with the admired or envied supervisor and then import aspects of the supervisor into the treatment (Sachs & Shapiro, 1976). We find it helpful to comment on the supervisee's behavior toward us if it illuminates or interferes with understanding the patient. Recurrent transference issues toward the supervisor or the patient may need to be referred for treatment if self-reflection by the supervisee is not sufficient to get past the difficulty.

Recognizing the tendency for trainees and supervisors to become vague, abstract, overly supportive, or critical of each other in response to the anxiety of the supervision setting, Szecsödy (1997) recommends managing the discomfort by the careful maintenance of the frame of supervision, analogous to the holding frame of therapy. He describes three aspects to the frame. First, the stationary aspect refers to the management of the learning environment in terms of time and place of meeting, payment, and methods of reporting. Second, the mobile aspect of the frame refers to the continuous, reflective review of the working relationship of therapist and supervisor. Finally, the focusing aspect of the frame concentrates on the patient–therapist interaction.

We enlarge the focus of the frame by reviewing the supervision process at a faculty meeting not only to improve our teaching but also to address the overlooked issue of how clinical skill is learned (Szecsödy, 1990). To the supervisor's report of progress and difficulties in supervision, other faculty members add their reviews of the student's way of working in previous supervision or in the small- and large-group at conferences. This generates a broader understanding of the student's learning process and development as a therapist. To our observations concerning the reflection of the therapy process in the supervisory relationship, we add that the nature of the therapist's contribution to the therapeutic relationship is reflected in the small- and large-group process. There is fractal similarity between the supervisee's patterns shown in therapeutic relationships, supervision, and group interaction.

In the example that follows, a supervisor describes her struggle to help an advanced woman student overcome a learning block that is preventing her from recognizing, gathering, and interpreting the transference. The woman is bright and affectively engaged, and so the faculty is puzzled as to why she has a learning block in this one area. We want to show how the supervisor thinks about the problems to be addressed in the supervision and how she is helped by input from faculty who know the student in other settings.

The supervisor describes the stages in the learning process and her use of faculty help as she and the woman work together on their blind and dumb spots supported by the learning matrix. Resistance and blocking give way to recognition of the transference. The example finishes with a brief follow-up on the supervisee's later work with the transference as a supervisor with her own supervisees.

Supervision for Adair

I was assigned as the third supervisor for Adair, a well-trained university teacher of graduate students in an analytically oriented social work school. Adair is highly motivated, well prepared, punctual, and well organized. She is nice, charming, beautiful, and kind. She knows analytic theory, and she is a senior clinician. She is thoroughly professional. Her patients make a good alliance with her, and they get symptomatic improvement. To an analyst, however, her clinical work lacks unconscious resonance. Perhaps others at the university sensed this, for she remained a classroom teacher and had not been authorized to do clinical supervision in the field.

The faculty discusses Adair's supervision needs

Adair was enrolled in the second year of the two-year program of affective learning and had chosen to have supervision as well. She had been in supervision with an individual supervisor and with a group supervisor. At a faculty meeting, her individual supervisor reported that he was frustrated in his attempts to help Adair. He asked the faculty for help. He said that Adair gave her clinical account in detail and then had nothing else to say. She could not free-associate to the material. He had done some free-association himself to show her how to do it, and she got better at letting thoughts come to her mind. He said that she tended to fill in the blanks with thoughts' but never with feelings.

One of the faculty who had been Adair's small-group leader commented that this fit with his impression. Adair had always formulated her thoughts on the concepts clearly and willingly, but she had tended not to share her emotional responses to the clinical material. Although she engaged in group discussions as a valued member, she did not bring in personal reactions linked to the group experience. He remained puzzled by his personal response of liking her very much but at the same time not feeling connected to her.

The supervisor responded by saying that it is easy to connect to Adair through the positive, but the negative is not there to relate to. That is what gives the feeling of something missing. The supervisor went on to tell the faculty that Adair is comfortable with the positive transference that goes along without interpretation but that she does not interpret, welcome, or even notice a negative transference. He said that he had learned that an influential teacher at the university had established a professional culture in which countertransference was always regarded as evidence of the therapist's infantile neurosis. He had the impression that Adair had been trained to suppress responses as if they were improper. The faculty agreed that when therapists learn in their formative years that personal reactions in the therapeutic context are always seen as pathological, it is hard to persuade them that countertransference is the centerpiece of treatment.

Then Adair's group supervisor spoke. In group supervision, he said, Adair was easily the most competent student and therefore was less aware of how much she had to learn than the others. The group supervisor felt that Adair's needs were getting lost. She recommended that Adair end the group supervision and concentrate on individual supervision. But the individual supervisor felt stymied. He valued Adair's mature personality, intelligence, commitment, and university experience, and he really wanted her clinical work to advance, but he felt thwarted in his attempts to work in the transference.

The faculty knew that Adair's working group wanted her to become a clinical supervisor, but no one could imagine that Adair could teach how to work with the transference if she could not work with it herself. The faculty thought that Adair was floating between two supervisions, neither of them taking hold of the problem. The faculty recommended concentrating the supervision effort in one place. They referred her to me, hoping that, with the information gathered from her previous individual and group supervisions and from her small-group experience, I could help Adair fill in the missing piece in her learning. My supervision task was to focus on helping Adair recognize and gather the transference and to use her countertransference as the fulcrum for transference interpretations.

Adair presented to me her individual therapy with two adult cases. The first was a middle-aged mother whose last child would soon leave for college. The second was a 23-year-old woman who had just left her mother to live independently. She chose to focus on the first case, the same one that she had had in supervision with the other supervisor.

Adair in supervision: case 1

Adair introduced the first case, the 45-year-old wife of a German diplomat and mother of two whose only son was about to leave home. Adair spelled out with medical precision the woman's four different types of medication that were prescribed for her during home leave in Germany. These are monitored by a local psychiatrist who also treats the husband. The woman has had a phobia of having sex with her husband since angrily suspecting him of an affair that he denied. If she finally had to be sexually involved with him, she froze. At times of extreme stress, she became quite disturbed. Adair's interpretation was that the woman tended to dissociate and become incoherent when she couldn't express the rage that she felt at her husband's continual lying and outrageous, neglectful behavior.

A missing countertransference

Adair had been away on vacation. She began supervision with me by reporting the first session with the patient after her return. She told me that the woman complained that her husband doesn't understand why she is not happy. He doesn't see that it's because of him. When Adair was away, he had upset her so much that she became incoherent. He's always asking why she's still in therapy and asking whether she will finish soon. When the woman became incoherent, he took her to his psychiatrist to diagnose her state of mind and get the proper medications, Adair reported all this to me in a calm, coherent, precise way.

> I started to make connections. Adair was away. Her patient became incoherent, Her patient thinks she is angry at her husband, but she has trouble expressing her anger. I'm thinking to myself, "The woman must also be angry at Adair who is away, and so she goes to a man to get the anger suppressed with medications, which her husband wants." I wanted to see whether Adair could make the connection, so I said, "Can you think about it some more? Why do you think she went to the psychiatrist?"
>
> Adair answered, "Her husband took her because he knows the psychiatrist, too. They used to see him for couple therapy, but the husband stopped going. When it happened once before, they went to that psychiatrist because he does a good job and he speaks German."

The more factual answers Adair gave me, the more upset I became. I was thinking that if my patient went to someone else, when I was away, I would definitely have questions. I might be upset to hear that she had trouble. I might be angry that she went to someone else. I might feel unsure of her commitment. I might feel guilty that I had not worked on this beforehand so it would not have happened. But not Adair. She was quite accepting of her patient's actions. Adair was completely calm, and I was completely upset.

> I said to Adair, "I find that I'm feeling upset by this, and I notice that you just accept the way it is. I'm just wondering why there would be this difference in our reactions?"
>
> She answered, "Well, he's not going to the couple therapy anymore."
>
> I couldn't see what that had to do with it. I simply asked Adair to tell me more.
>
> She continued, "And I know that the patient has a strong tie to me, so why would I worry if she goes to the psychiatrist?"
>
> I said that since the tie was strong, separation must mean something to the woman. I asked Adair what had been discussed about her impending vacation. She told me that, naturally, she would

expect the woman to go to the psychiatrist she and her husband already knew. What Adair said made sense in practical terms, but I felt uncomfortable with the reasoning and the certainty. I realized that my main discomfort was not so much with the specifics of the arrangement as with Adair's total neglect of the issue of separation and attachment.

Adair then explained to me, "The patient likes to talk a lot, so if I'm not here to talk to, she'd want to go talk to the psychiatrist. And, in a way, the psychiatrist is better because he speaks the patient's native language, so the patient can tell him things she might not want to tell me. She forgets she has told them to him and not to me."

There is a split in the transference here that Adair is quite accepting of and not concerned about because she is so sure of the woman's basic attachment to her. Adair is unable to see or to think about any difficulty that mars the positive transference. This is a blind spot.

Adair said, "So do you want me to tell you about the next session?"

And I said, "No, I can't go on. If this happened to me, I tell you, I'd be really upset."

She said, "No, I wasn't. I was grateful there was someone she could trust that she could turn to."

That made sense. It sounded mature and generous. I felt ridiculous. Why was I upset? I thought it over. As the supervisor, I hadn't seen the patient, and I didn't know whether she really needed medications. I didn't know whether this was the best referral for her. What I did know was that Adair was accepting practical explanations rather than searching for emotional meanings. I began to think of how to help Adair get more in touch with the emotions of the transference.

"Tell me again how you understand what is happening," I suggested.

Adair gave me her formulation. "This woman dissociates the feeling from the situation she is in, and she blocks being close. She doesn't want to get too attached to her husband. She can't really express anger at her husband, who is always traveling. It reminds

her of when her father left. She doesn't want to suffer. So, really the
main issue is a blocking of anger. That's makes her feel crazy. And
that's why she takes the medications."

What Adair said made sense. It was not formulaic. It was a sophisti-
cated understanding of the woman's dynamics. I respected that, and it
fit with my estimation of her advanced level of training. But it was not
emotionally engaged. I began to wonder whether Adair was relieved
that the woman has a psychiatrist to go to who will give her a substitute
attachment of a person from home and a drug so that she doesn't get so
angry that she goes crazy.

At this stage in our supervision work together, the closest thing to an
interpretation that Adair reported was saying to her patient, "You were
upset that your husband went away, and it felt overwhelming because
it reminded you of when your father went away. It's a re-creation of
the trauma of that early separation." This seemed correct, but it totally
ignored the related information that Adair was gone on vacation for
three weeks. The connections were not being made to the transference.
I realized that Adair was not having the feelings I would expect a therapist to have. The countertransference was not being experienced. It was
being projected, perhaps into the patient and certainly into me.

If this were therapy, I might conceptualize this problem in terms of
a resistance or an impenetrable defense against a childhood trauma of
some kind. But in supervision, I find a different orientation helpful. I saw
Adair's difficulty as a failure of notation (Bion, 1962). She could not
notate the *selected facts* that I presented to her concerning work with the
transference. She could not see that the patient's anger at her husband
served to prevent her from recognizing her anger at Adair for being
away. She could not notate her own emotional response to the patient's
flight to a new object. While unable to notate these facts, she was, however, able to project her countertransference into me. My introjective
identification allows me to notate her countertransference and describe
the patient's transference, which makes a start toward understanding.
But Adair's failure of notation blocks that understanding, and I cannot
get verification of the validity of the fact.

Working with my countertransference got us nowhere. It just
increased the distance between us. Presenting the carefully thought-out
facts did not help. So I had to avoid thinking and analyzing and simply
ask Adair how she felt about whatever the patient might say or do.

Blocking the transference to absence

In a session after another vacation some months later, Adair was still dealing with the woman's rage at her husband. She reported that the woman said that he was outrageous, that he was like her father, and that she was as angry with him as she had been the day she heard that her parents were to be divorced. Adair convinced me that the husband had earned her patient's righteous anger. But the thread of the associations this time tied the woman's rage to what just happened in the therapeutic relationship, as it always did, especially obvious at times when Adair had been away or was about to go away. Again, it was obvious to me but not to Adair.

> I asked, "Don't you see the thread? The woman is worried that when you go away you'll be leaving her so as to avoid her and her craziness that her husband can't stand and that you'll be going off to have a trip with your husband, who wants to be with you. You and he are the couple she's referring to when she tells you how enraged she was when she heard her parents were having a divorce."
>
> Adair replied, "Well, that's interesting to think about, but I'm not convinced. Because when her husband is away, she feels free."
>
> I thought to myself, "When Adair is away, she must imagine that the patient is feeling free. Therefore, she won't have to feel guilty. She can't imagine herself being with her husband causing this reaction. So she blocks the communication and blocks the connection."

Although I could think my way through this more easily at this stage of our working together, I felt hopeless about saying any of it. I felt that Adair blocks, blocks, blocks. It was hard for me to deal with. I began to think that there was a treatment issue here, but that was not it. Adair was a well-adjusted, likable person with a stable family life and no inhibitions. Her own attachments to friends, family, and colleagues were strong and devoted. Everyone liked her. I went back to thinking over the material. Adair did not harvest the split-off, regressive, dissociated fragments that got put into the mother tongue and left with the psychiatrist. When the patient got very depressed and sounded fragmented, Adair stood by while she sent herself to the psychiatrist, who squashed it. There was nothing wrong with Adair's ability to feel empathy for her patient and to resonate with her rage at the object.

Perhaps she got scared of the underlying sadness and craziness and had to block it.

As I thought of this blocking, Adair now said that when she gives one of her formulations, the patient blocks it and cuts her off somehow. I said to Adair, "The woman is worried about being disconnected from the person she's attached to, her husband, and she freezes him out. I think she's also worried about you leaving. This separation anxiety gets acted out as a cutting off of your ideas. The disconnect happens now, before you actually leave her."

Adair replied, "Yes, but I've been through more difficult ideas than this with her."

I said, "Adair this *is* the difficult idea, and I feel you are cutting it off with me." Having pointed out the fractal similarity between the therapeutic and the supervisory process, I said, "Now I'm thinking about how to deal with this with you. How am I going to get to this?"

I talked with her about what was happening between her and me, thinking that she would learn to do that with her patient. But it worked no better this time than it had before. So I resolved to return to my earlier strategy of asking how she feels about things. I followed my intention at first, but then I reverted. "In the transference material about her husband never listening, constantly traveling, and telling her to take her medication, we can see the transference. She doesn't want to give you her feelings because she's afraid you'll banish her or maybe send her to another therapist."

Adair responded, "Yes, she's angry at her husband and at her last therapist." Adair confirmed the value of the idea of displacement of the transference to her, but the idea of gathering the transference to herself was cut off again.

I said, "You know that this woman is full of fury and despair. Right now she thinks of you as a good object in a sea of mistrust and disappointment. But rage is such an issue for her, it's bound to be directed at you at some point if you manage not to block it. And when that happens, you might possibly get filled with it, and it may spill over in relation to me. So if you notice stirrings of angry feelings towards me, please talk about them."

Well, of course, she didn't, but I made it clear that this could happen.

In response to my comment, Adair showed that she connected anger at the husband to anger at the previous therapist but not to herself. Now we have established the connection between craziness, anger, interrupted attachment, and anger at a therapist. But I was always left with the feeling that the pieces weren't coming together. Adair said things that were absolutely right on, and yet there was this disconnect.

The inability to recognize the impact of absence continued even when premature termination came into view. Adair found out that her patient would have to move back to Europe in six months because her husband was being reassigned to fill a vacant diplomatic post. In the months following this announcement, there were many missed sessions because of travel to Europe for interviews. Adair reported many details of their discussion about whether the patient and her husband would be sent to this country or that country in Europe, which type of residence they would prefer, which college to select for their son, whether he should be educated in the United States like his sister, or in Europe where his parents would be, and so on. I was getting the facts but none of the emotion.

> I asked Adair, "What do you feel as you face losing her?"
>
> Adair said, "Well, I'm just feeling I haven't done enough for her."
>
> I said, "I'm feeling like you. I can't do enough for you. And I really want to help you because you are so good in so many ways."

Support from the learning matrix

In a faculty meeting, now six months after beginning my work with Adair, I described the problem. A colleague pointed out that my feelings about Adair mirrored those of her previous supervisor. Some faculty members were filled with the sense of hopelessness and frustration that I was conveying. Others felt that there was some progress in that Adair was now able to link the patient's reaction to her husband with anger toward the patient's previous therapist. On the other hand, she could not see her patient's anger as transference to herself, she could not see her countertransference, and she could not relate to my fractal image of the countertransference in the supervisory relationship.

Adair was getting closer, but there was still a long way to go. One of her small-group leaders said that he had had the same experience of Adair being so close and yet so far from getting it. Her former supervisor suggested that the block of Adair's career path was causing her to block her thinking. Perhaps he had a point, but I knew that until her thinking was freed up, her career path would not open up either. I said to the faculty group, "Adair will never be a supervisor until she can put the elements of the transference together in her clinical work," The group shared my dilemma of how to go about enabling this to happen. While the group was talking, I felt encouraged, and suddenly I knew what to do. I should tell Adair in a positive tone that to be a supervisor she needed to learn how to work in the transference and that I was working toward that goal.

> I went back to the next supervision session and told Adair, "You are so good at so many aspects of therapeutic work. If you could just get this transference piece of therapeutic skill, the whole thing would come together, and you could be a clinical supervisor." Adair said that she really wanted to get it and that she would try.

First recognition of the transference

> In the next supervision session, Adair reported the patient's ruminations on details about the move, the uprooting, the house relocation, the planting, and the furnishing of the new residence. Adair concluded, "She is her husband's entire support system, so she has to go arrange the move, buy the house, furnish it, and replant the garden. Now that he's leaving, she has to go uproot. She's missing this place so much, and she's feeling overwhelmed at how much she will have to do to re-create a home and a beautiful garden."
>
> Then Adair said to me, "You know what she said? She said, 'I wish I could take my orchids with me.' This was really amazing because *I* love orchids too, and I have them in my office. So I knew what she meant, I said, 'Maybe you wish you could take me, too.' Then she started laughing, and she said, 'I know it's impossible.' And so we started talking about how to transfer her to another therapist once she gets there. But she wants to get the details of the move settled first."

When Adair recognized the patient's longing to keep her with her, I experienced a glimmer of hope that Adair had got it. Here was a flicker of recognition that confirmed that Adair had taken in what I had been saying. But she let go of it quickly. When she switched to the topic of referral, I felt that the transference was cut off again. Even so, I felt some excitement that I carried in to the next supervision session.

Obliterating the transference

In another session, the patient expressed negative feelings that I thought clearly contained her transference to Adair. So I said to Adair, "Here is another opportunity for recognizing and gathering the transference."

This time Adair said, "No. I really don't think it's there. When I supervised this case with my first supervisor, there really were far more frequent transference issues. They're not really in the material here."

I said, "Adair, I know you don't see it. But if I see it, I have to show it to you, and I will continue to do that."

I realized that the positive transference was now in Adair's line of vision but not the negative transference. I looked for an intervention that expressed my positive transference toward Adair as a clinician and at the same time showed her the negative side. The comment that I was about to make was actually almost the same as the one that the faculty had encouraged me to say. I had said it already, but this time I said it more directly, with greater conviction, and at a core-affective moment.

I said, "The reason I keep going after this is that we find you to be a very senior clinician and teacher, and this is a little piece that is missing. For you to be a clinical supervisor, which is something that we really want for you, you need to get this piece of understanding. You can't do this work at your best until you've got it."

Adair responded positively to this. I think it really helped her to listen to me when I said that I needed her to achieve her full potential rather than asking her to recognize and make up a deficiency. I related to her through the acceptable positive transference in order to have her become an attractor for organizing the negative transference.

Before we could complete the supervision task, the patient terminated. I talked with Adair about where we had gotten to in supervision. Adair was still using the psychiatrist to deal with the depression medically, she was still unconvinced about the transference, and she still neglected to interpret the impact of her absences and the patient's premature termination. Adair did now interpret the patient's positive transference, but she still could not see the negative transference. Unhinged from its aggressive counterpart, the positive transference to Adair operated like an exciting object relationship that then left the patient at the mercy of her rejecting object relationships. I sensed some improvement in the recognition of transference but not enough. All the same, I felt encouraged that I could approach her blind spot from this area of enlarging vision.

Adair in supervision: case 2

I asked Adair to find another case that was ongoing. I said that my goal would be to intensify our focus on learning from the countertransference and recognizing the transference. I knew that Adair would need me to come at it indirectly.

Adair's second case was a young woman with a depressed, suicidal, raging, intrusive, violent mother and a remote, neglectful, intellectual father. Her boyfriend treated her badly. The mother was psychotic, the father was absent, and the boyfriend was hopeless. The young woman was trying to win the right to live independently.

Adair's account of her treatment conveyed the tumult and crisis in the young woman's family relationships—my mother this, my father that, I'm going to college, I'm quitting my job, my boss is abusing me, frantic phone calls, horrible emergencies, mother's intrusive phone calls, boyfriend's cheating, and so on. I felt overwhelmed by the material, but Adair remained steady and supportive. She did not draw any negative expressions toward herself. Adair made good interpretations more frequently now. She saw that this young woman's abusive relationship with her boyfriend repeated the experience of being with a disturbed mother who abused her. Adair's observing ego was continuing to develop, but a fully engaging, affective ego was still missing.

So much of this young woman's material had to be full of transference, but now I couldn't see it either.

> I said to Adair, "I can't find the transference in this. It's got to be there, but there's so much material, all of it urgent, realistic, and external. There are so many awful things going on. There are no dreams to help us. I just can't see it."

I had set my aim at working with transference, but the case that Adair chose was overwhelming my preferred way of working. I asked the faculty meeting for help again. One of my colleagues wondered why Adair would choose that case and suggested that perhaps she wanted to try to keep me away from the transference as well. Adair's former supervisor noted that she had presented a similarly disorganized situation to him. Another colleague had the idea that the young woman's transference was to the total situation. She deposited that with Adair, who then conveyed it to me without metabolizing it because of not sensing the negative transference. Someone else pointed out that Adair's self was gratified by being able to locate badness in the object. Again I said that I couldn't understand why the material bothered me more than it bothered her, and I wondered whether she was really far more bothered about it than she showed.

The man who had been her individual supervisor thought that Adair might be completely terrified about being in touch with anger in her therapeutic relationships. He reminded me that the culture at the university was to suppress emotions. Perhaps Adair was afraid that if she showed an intense feeling, I would pathologize it. But she knew that I didn't think that way. After all, I had shared my feelings of upset when her first woman patient referred herself to a psychiatrist instead of working on her grief and rage in the transference. Adair gave me the impression that there was no need for anyone to feel that upset about it. Talking about this challenge with my colleagues gave me more distance from the problem. I began to think more positively about my progress in confronting the learning difficulty.

It was clear to me and to Adair that this young woman valued her sessions highly. Adair did nothing intrusive or hurtful toward the young woman. On the contrary, she was solicitous, was responsive to occasional phone calls, and sometimes gave advice that was based on maternal feelings of wanting the best for her. The young woman's mother was so destructive that Adair was wonderful in comparison, the kind of mother to have. Adair did see the positive transference. For example, she recognized the transference significance of the patient's reference to a sum of money that was approximately twice Adair's therapy fee. Adair made the inference that the woman was wanting to see her twice a week instead of once. This told me that she recognized the positive transference but didn't know to remark on it. She used the positive transference to the patient's advantage, but she could not think about it. Not being able to make transference thinkable, she could not note it as a selected fact, and therefore she could not take the next step of interpreting it.

The patient continued to have so much to say and so much to do. This meant that there was always a long story for Adair to tell me, a passing through from Adair to me of the patient's transference to Adair as a willing ear, a sponge—an attentive, detoxifying mother, one who must not comment on the negative transference for fear of identifying herself with the abusive mother.

Affect enters the supervision

I had not met with Adair the previous week because she was on vacation. She began the next session by reporting the usual kind of material. The young woman told her that the boyfriend doesn't have enough time for her, the boyfriend doesn't understand her, and the boyfriend changes the plans. The young woman was angry with him, but not as angry as he was. He was so angry with her for what he imagined that she had done to him that he went off with another woman. She thought that she would have to break up with him because he was in such a rage.

> This reminded me of Adair's first patient, who fled to a new object. I said to Adair, "I think the patient is talking about the boyfriend's anger instead of talking about her own anger, not just at him but also at you because you were on vacation again. Tell me, why would she need to do this?"
>
> Adair replied, "She doesn't want the other person to get angry with her. She wants the other person to care about her and her family."

I noted that Adair's answer came through in the displacement. She resonated with the tendency to focus on what the other person will do or feel, but at least she was acknowledging someone's fear of being the recipient of negative feeling.

> I said, "Look Adair, she's telling you how you shouldn't leave her. She's saying, 'Look how upset people get when they are dropped or when someone is off with someone else instead of the person they've abandoned.'"
>
> Adair said, "I agree with you. Yes, I agree with you."
>
> Adair accepted it this time. It still felt as if she had been persuaded intellectually, until suddenly she said, full of feeling, "I know I'm really all she's got."

That was a big move for Adair. To me, that was gratifying. I realized that she was still more in touch with need, attachment, and love than with frustration, rejection, and hate, but now I felt that we would get there, too.

The moment of "getting it"

Now that Adair was in touch with affect and recognizing that she functions best in an intellectual mode, I gave her material to read about the transference (J. Scharff & D. Scharff, 1998b). Adair did her homework.

> Adair said, "I've thought a lot about transference, countertransference, and the therapeutic instrument. And now I've got it!"
>
> I was skeptical, and I waited for the proof in her clinical account.
>
> Adair continued describing the young woman's thoughts and her own responses, saying, "She complained to me that she had been in therapy a longtime and the problems were still there. I said, 'I think that you're thinking and feeling that I'm not doing enough to help you.' The woman said, 'Yes.' And I said, 'Talk to me more about this.'"

"Talk to me more about this"! How many times I had used those very words to her! It was gratifying to hear her use them with her patient and encourage the expression of negative feeling. Indeed she had got it, but I waited to see whether it would remain with her and not get cut off.

In the next supervision session, Adair reported that the young woman talked about how horrible her reality is, how alone she feels, and how she hopes for a prince to save her. She described fully how hard it is for her when Adair goes on vacation.

The patient was in a direct discussion of the transference, and I looked to see how Adair dealt with it.

> Adair said to me, "Do you think she's relating this fantasy of a savior-prince to me?"
>
> I said, "Yes, I do. I think she sees you not just as a good mother but now as a prince who could rescue her."
>
> Adair said to me, "So you see, I really can see the transference now." And I said, "Yes, I think you can." I asked Adair what she thought was in the way of it before.
>
> Adair replied, "I really couldn't believe that it was about me. I didn't want to feel grandiose. But now I see I'm just an instrument."

Now it was my turn to have an insight. Adair taught me something about resistance to working in the transference. Some people may feel that they cannot matter that much to somebody. Others may imagine that they are displacing the real objects in a patient's life by becoming transference objects and diminishing the reality of the original objects.

Using the term *instrument* might suggest reaching out cognitively into the material rather than containing it, but this use of the term appealed to me because it captured the sense of the therapist as a tool used by the patient in getting the work done (Fleming & Benedek, 1966; J. Scharff & D. Scharff, 1998c). I do think that Adair was demonstrating a containing function. What she was gathering in the transference was becoming more tolerable, more able to be thought and felt. Adair proved to me that she could now see the positive and the negative transference. Nevertheless, the emotions she was able to connect with were still mostly in the area of need, idealization, and longing. As an instrument for receiving rage, Adair was not yet finely tuned. Still the winds of change were blowing, and the next step would be to help her make her transference interpretations directly to the patient.

Interpreting the transference

Now that she understood and accepted her importance to the patient, Adair rapidly became able to interpret the transference significance of her patient's destructive relationships.

The young woman got involved in a highly destructive, humiliating reunion with her ex-boyfriend the next time Adair was away. When sessions resumed, the young woman was ashamed and felt like quitting treatment. Adair recognized that this was not just the patient's turning to a boyfriend with whom to repeat the abuse she suffered from her mother. She now realized that this was her patient's way of letting her know how desperate she felt when Adair was on vacation, as if to say, "See what happens when you leave me."

At last, the turning of anger at the object against the self was delivered into the treatment situation, and Adair interpreted it thoroughly. Once the patient was able to acknowledge and work through her anger at Adair, she became able to find a better job and a new boyfriend who treated her with respect. But the young woman found that she did not find this decent young man sexually appealing. Adair knew that sexual guilt was troubling this patient, but she tended to accept the patient's resistance to discussing her sexuality. When Adair pressed the issue, with my encouragement, the young woman expressed a lot of anger at people in her life, so that the topic of sex was not addressed.

> Adair reported, "I said to the patient, 'The anger you are feeling about everybody takes up all the time and diverts us from discussing sexual feelings. I think you are angry at me for raising this issue because you are afraid of looking bad in front of me.'"

Adair now not only saw the transference but also understood how to use it as the fulcrum for change.

Adair as the supervisor

I was pleased to learn that the university promoted Adair to a clinical supervisory role. She presented two of her individual supervision cases to me. She did an excellent job of establishing a good alliance with her supervisees and asking them to look at transference manifestations. She was particularly good at helping her supervisees notice their enactments of good-mother transferences that covered over bad-mother identifications. She discussed with me her observations and her strategies for how to approach problem areas. I was especially gratified to notice how often she asked her supervisees to tell her more, to tell her what feelings the patients aroused, and to ask them to look at the transference. She told me that she is glad that she is now better able to accept rage expressed toward her in the transference and is still working on it. I was gratified when Adair told me that learning in supervision had convinced her to work on dealing more directly with her own anger as a therapist and a teacher.

When colleagues read this chapter, they confirmed that they had noticed the same changes in her group participation. They agreed that Adair had recovered from her state of faulty notation. The blind spot was no longer there.

When Adair read this chapter, she gave her own view of what made the difference in her ability to see the transference. She said:

> "I couldn't see it before because I didn't know how to think it. All the supervisions helped me a lot, but they hadn't gotten me to notice the transference. I wish you could have just given me concrete examples or told me what I was doing wrong and shown me how to do it right. I didn't know that I was looking in the wrong place. I was still looking for transference as the patient experiencing me as a re-edition of a particular family member. Recognizing the countertransference was easy because I know what I feel, but I couldn't find the transference in it because I never believe that my feelings have that much importance."
>
> "Sometimes I need something concrete. So reading the paper on how to think about the geography of the transference helped me (J. Scharff & D. Scharff, 1998b). Then in supervision I got it! You wanted me to take my feelings, connect them to the theme of the session, and see how my feelings and the theme were expressing the patient's hidden thoughts and feelings about me. So then I knew what to look for and what to do. It was when the second patient was able to admit to her feelings about me that I finally got it. It has made a tremendous difference in my work with patients and students and in my group. I can see it even helps me in my own family."

References

Arlow, J. (1963). The supervisory situation. *Journal of the American Psychoanalytic Association, 11*: 576–594.

Bion, W. R. (1962). *Learning from Experience.* New York: Basic Books.

Fleming, J. & Benedek, T. (1966). *Psychoanalytic Supervision: A Method of Clinical Teaching.* New York: Gruner and Stratton.

Gleick, J. (1987). *Chaos.* New York: Viking.

Sachs, D. M. & Shapiro, S. H. (1976). On parallel processes in therapy and teaching. *Psychoanalytic Quarterly, 45*: 394–415.

Scharff, D. (1998). Chaos theory and self-organizing systems. Paper presented at "Separation Anxiety and Psychoanalysis" conference, International Institute of Object Relations Therapy (re-named the International Psychotherapy Institute www.theipi.org), Bethesda, MD, December.

Scharff, D. (2000). The taming of psychological chaos: Fairbairn and self-organizing systems. Paper presented at "Fairbairn and Relational Theory Today" Lisbon October. Reprinted as Fairbairn and the self as an organized system: Chaos theory as a new paradigm. In: *Fairbairn and Relational Theory Today*, ed. F. Fereira & D. E. Scharff, pp. 197–211. London: Karnac.

Scharff, J. S. & Scharff, D. E. (1998a). Chaos theory and fractals in development, self and object relations, and development. In: *Object Relations Individual Therapy*, pp. 153–182. Northvale, NJ: Jason Aronson.

Scharff, J. S. & Scharff, D. E. (1998b). Geography of transference and countertransference. In: *Object Relations Individual Therapy*, pp. 241–281. Northvale, NJ: Jason Aronson.

Scharff, J. S. & Scharff, D. E. (1998c). *Object Relations Individual Therapy.* Northvale, NJ: Jason Aronson.

Searles, H. (1965). Problems of psychoanalytic supervision.. In *Collected Papers on Schizophrenia and Related Topics*, pp. 584–604. Madison, CT and New York: International Universities Press.

Szecsödy, I. (1990). *The Learning Process in Psychotherapy Supervision.* Stockholm Karolinska Institute.

Szecsödy, I. (1997). Framing the psychoanalytic frame. *Scandinavian Psychoanalytic Review, 20*: 238–243.

INDEX